D0939011

FIGHTING
FEAR

Other books by the author:

The Seclusion Room

Maneuvers

Caring: Home Treatment for the Emotionally Disturbed

FIGHTING FEAR

An Eight-Week Guide to
Treating Your Own Phobias

Fredric Neuman, M.D.

Macmillan Publishing Company

New York

852407

Missouri Western State College
Hearnes Learning Resources Center
4525 Downs Drive
St. Joseph, Missouri 64507

Copyright © 1985 by Fredric Neuman, M.D.

All rights reserved. No part of this book may be reproduced or transmitted in any form or by any means, electronic or mechanical, including photocopying, recording or by any information storage and retrieval system, without permission in writing from the Publisher.

Macmillan Publishing Company
866 Third Avenue, New York, N.Y. 10022
Collier Macmillan Canada, Inc.

Library of Congress Cataloging in Publication Data
Neuman, Fredric.
    Fighting fear.
    Bibliography: p.
    1. Phobias—Treatment.   2. Behavior therapy.
I. Title.
RC535.N48   1985   616.85′225   85-4897
ISBN 0-02-590910-X

Macmillan books are available at special discounts for bulk purchases for sales promotions, premiums, fund-raising, or educational use. For details, contact:

Special Sales Director
Macmillan Publishing Company
866 Third Avenue
New York, N.Y. 10022

10 9 8 7 6 5 4 3 2 1

Designed by Jack Meserole

Printed in the United States of America

This book is not intended as a substitute for the medical advice of your own physician. The reader should regularly consult a physician in matters relating to his or her health and particularly in respect of any symptoms that may require diagnosis or medical attention.

Contents

Acknowledgments

I wish to thank, first of all, those patients who participated in the eight-week clinic upon which this book is based. Prior to participation and before the results of treatment could be known, each patient agreed to allow recordings of our meetings to be made and used along with the case histories in this teaching program.* I am similarly indebted to the phobia aides and to the co-leader of the clinic. I would also like to thank the administrative staff of the Department of Psychiatry of White Plains Hospital and especially that of the Phobia Clinic itself. Their dedication and enthusiasm has accounted, as much as any other factor, for the success and growing reputation of the clinic. Doreen Powell and Joanne Antonelli provided useful suggestions to the organization of this particular clinic. Doug French helped analyze some of the statistical information. I would like to express my special appreciation to Dr. Manuel D. Zane, who designed and founded the Phobia Clinic. His ideas underlie much of what is done here. Certain principles of treatment, taken for granted now in the management of phobic disorders, originated with him. Inevitably, though, each worker in the field develops his own particular point of view, laying special emphasis on what he thinks is especially important. Dr. Zane should not be held accountable, therefore, for what I say or have neglected to say here. Finally, I have to express my admiration for the

* Those wishing to obtain this home-centered treatment program in its entirety, including these tapes, can receive the necessary information from the White Plains Hospital Phobia Clinic or directly from me.

many phobic patients I have seen these last twenty years. To those who have come to know them well, and to know their struggle, their courage and determination are inspiring.

Introduction

I developed an interest in phobias, and in agoraphobia in particular, in 1954, as the result of developing the condition myself. One day without any evident reason I became panicky. I had the feeling I was going to go crazy or scream or in some way lose control of myself. It was a dramatic and inexplicable feeling. It was obvious, I thought, that something terrible was the matter with me. After leafing through the pages of my college psychology textbook (I was in college at the time), I tentatively decided I was suffering from an anxiety reaction, a neurotic depression, probably, a panic state also, and a variety of other illnesses—possibly including schizophrenia. In the opinion of my roommate, I was also a hypochondriac. But my readiness to see myself as ill in all sorts of ways was not solely an expression of my suddenly heightened concern about myself. There is indeed an overlap among some of these conditions and also a tendency by different clinicians to call the same illness by different names. I would have chosen to settle the matter by seeing a psychiatrist—hoping along the way to get cured—but I was concerned that being on record as emotionally ill would hurt my chances of being accepted into medical school. That would not be so, the physician at the student health service told me when I asked, unless I was suffering from a "character disorder." But I naturally assumed that I had a character disorder, whatever that was, along with everything else. So I lived with the condition for the next few years—with considerable difficulty, as everyone does—and along the way stumbled over the principles of treatment that allowed me finally to get well. These methods have been independently advanced and reformulated by a number of different investigators. By now they constitute the standard, conventional treatment of phobic and panic states. As usual, everyone has a name for his own particular method, but most commonly this sort of treatment—exemplified in this eight-week clinic—is called behavior therapy or, more specifically, exposure therapy.

Most serious phobias are variants of agoraphobia, a troublesome condition. Someone so affected may be incapacitated. And it is difficult to treat for one principal reason: The phobic person no longer believes he or she can be helped. Understandably. Such a person is likely to have been subjected over the course of his illness to an extraordinary variety of diagnostic procedures—everything from brain scans and hair analyses to cardiac catheterization, including especially glucose tolerance tests and other determinations of endocrine function—all to no benefit. Very likely he * has been told he was suffering from any of a great variety of physical or mental disorders—everything I could imagine as a naive college student, and more. Very many phobics have been diagnosed as having hypoglycemia —almost always in error. On the other hand, they may have been told also they had nothing at all the matter with them. Whatever the diagnosis, most of these patients have been treated previously. Even those thought to have nothing the matter with them were likely to have been offered some kind of treatment, usually drugs, often one of the minor tranquilizers, but also diets of various sorts, hypnosis, techniques of muscle relaxation, meditation, and so on. Occasionally someone may have been hospitalized, sometimes for considerable periods of time. Success has been reported with these different modalities of treatment and

* Rather than repeat over and over again "he or she," I will adhere to the convention of using the masculine pronoun, despite the fact that four out of five agoraphobics are women. What I have to say, in any case, applies equally to both sexes.

others, including psychoanalysis, but the failure rate is very high. Therefore, most patients, having been treated at different times by different doctors for different disorders, *and having failed to improve*, become discouraged and disbelieving of anyone who offers to embroil them in still one more method of treatment. It is just this cynicism and hopelessness that makes treatment difficult. The proper treatment of phobias is not easy at best, and entering into it halfheartedly makes success unlikely. In short, getting well depends as much on morale as on anything else. The patient has to keep trying long enough to succeed.

As for my own illness, it receded slowly after considerable and painful effort, then went away entirely. I became a doctor and then a psychiatrist. My interest in these disorders remained, however, and I found that I was seeing more than my share of such patients. Ten years ago I was invited to join the staff of the White Plains Hospital Phobia Clinic by Dr. Manuel D. Zane, its director and founder. Over six hundred patients have been treated at this clinic, and through questionnaires, newsletters, and contact with other physicians around the country who specialize in the treatment of phobias, we have knowledge of thousands of such patients. *The great majority of these patients report themselves—and indeed seem to be—markedly improved by proper treatment.*

I give this account of myself and the experience of the phobia clinic for two reasons: To indicate plainly that there is reason to be optimistic about treatment. Among those greatly improved or cured are some who have been seriously phobic for twenty or thirty years, sometimes to the point of being housebound. And to indicate that it is possible for someone working solely by himself or with a helper to get well. There is reason to be optimistic even for those who have failed repeatedly in previous treatments.

In order to get well only two things must be learned:

1. The phobic person can confront those situations of which he is afraid, safely, without embarrassing himself and without running away.
2. The feeling of panic itself can be mastered.

In theory it is a simple program but in practice, unfortunately, it is very difficult. At every point along the way of treatment there are obstacles. This book is an attempt to address these difficulties.

There is, however, a commonsense caveat I wish to make explicit. The suggestions I offer on these pages were made originally to patients known to me. The remarks I addressed to them are what I would say to anyone suffering from an uncomplicated phobia. But there are indeed both physical and emotional disorders that can present what seem at first to be phobic symptoms. For example, there are middle-ear conditions that cause dizziness, cardiac conditions (such as mitral valve prolapse) that cause arrhythmias, and even—rarely—hypoglycemia that can cause weakness and tremulousness, along with a whole array of other more serious symptoms. An agitated depression is frequently confused with a phobia. This illness responds well usually to antidepressant medication and not to behavior therapy. It is important, therefore, in the treatment of phobic disorders—as in the treatment of any medical condition—to be certain it is indeed that condition from which the patient is suffering. Each patient deserves an evaluation by a properly trained psychiatrist or psychologist. *Nothing I have set down here can be interpreted as an explicit prescription for patients I have not seen.*

About the White Plains Hospital Phobia Clinic

The White Plains Hospital Phobia Clinic began in 1971 on the initiative of and under the direction of Manuel D. Zane, one of the first psychoanalytically trained psychiatrists actually to accompany phobic patients into those situations threatening to them. The first eight-week program offered by the clinic was a combination of group and exposure therapy and was among the first of its kind offered anywhere in the country. Its obvious success led to a rapid expansion of services. Patients suffering from all kinds of phobias were treated. Once they had recovered, a number went on to be trained formally by the clinic as phobia aides. Some aides set up phobia clinics of their own, as did many other professionals, including psychiatrists and psychologists who were trained by the clinic. As a result, the ideas that underlie exposure therapy have been disseminated widely.

Among the various services offered at present by the White Plains Hospital Phobia Clinic are the following:

1. *The Eight-Week Program* through which over six hundred patients have received treatment.
2. *The Intensive Course* for those who live at a distance but who could take daily treatment by traveling to White Plains for one or two weeks.
3. *Self-help groups* in which three thousand patients have participated.
4. *Telephone clinics and outreach programs* for those so constrained by their phobias that they are unable to leave their houses.

5. *A newsletter* with current printings in excess of seven hundred copies, designed to maintain communication among phobic persons and to report differing theories and therapies.

In addition, there are training programs for the purpose of instructing professionals and paraprofessionals in the techniques required to work with phobics.

Because of the widespread publicity attending the work of the clinic, including more than one hundred newspaper and magazine articles and a segment on *60 Minutes*, more than eight thousand unsolicited letters from phobics have been received requesting help or advice. This overwhelming response lends credence to recent statistical surveys that suggest phobias are among the most common of all psychiatric disorders.

FIGHTING
FEAR

Chapter 1

PHOBIAS

A phobia is an excessive or unreasonable fear that leads a person to avoid a particular object or situation. For example, someone who is afraid of elevators, who is continually preoccupied by the thought that somehow he will be trapped in an elevator with some awful result and who therefore refuses to go into an elevator, can be said to have an elevator phobia. Such fears are unrealistic but tend to persist nevertheless, despite reassurance. Phobias are common and diverse. Coming across a new phobia, a physician responds first, naturally, by giving it a Greek or Latinate name. Hence ailurophobia is a fear of cats, algophobia a fear of pain, mysophobia* a fear of germs, and panphobia a fear of everything. And so on. Unfortunately, putting a name to an illness is not the same as explaining it. These descriptive terms fail even to describe adequately. Phobias merge into each other so that someone afraid to drive over bridges is also likely to be afraid of traveling in buses or planes, or shopping in supermarkets, or attending elaborate social affairs such as weddings. And

---

* Some so-called phobias, a germ phobia being one example, are really obsessions, one expression of an obsessive-compulsive neurosis. The two illnesses are distinguished in part by the nature of the discomfort they engender in the affected person; panic in the phobic; a kind of uneasy revulsion in the compulsive. Both conditions respond to behavior therapy, although phobias more readily, in my experience.

where exactly someone experiences fear is not crucial, anyway, to understanding the condition. What matters is the whole sum of feelings the person experiences and the coping mechanisms, always including avoidance, with which he deals with those feelings. Phobias—those severe enough to be of concern—are complicated clinical syndromes marked by psychological and physiological disturbances, and also disturbances of attitude and behavior. They are founded, in part at least, on mistakes in learning that have grown over a period of years. These ideas seem after a while to have a life of their own. They cause, and in turn grow out of, maladaptive behavior, ways of coping that tend to worsen the condition. This much can probably be said about any emotional disorder. They have complex roots in the past and give evidence of themselves in the present in many different aspects of the affected person's state of mind and in his actions.

There are relatively discrete phobias. It is possible, for instance, for someone to be afraid of snakes and manage to live comfortably simply by avoiding snakes. However such a phobia may have started, whether out of a misunderstanding about the actual dangerousness of snakes or because of some unconscious, symbolic meaning snakes may have come to represent, or for whatever reason, the snake phobia remains, at least in some cases, just that; a fear of snakes. The fear does not spread to other objects or circumstances, and the individual's life is not impaired to any great extent. Other such "simple" phobias are the following:

- Insects, especially flying insects such as moths and most especially stinging insects such as bees or wasps
- Rodents, especially rats
- Birds, especially pigeons
- Dogs or, less commonly, cats
- Snakes
- Sharks

These various creatures are not necessarily frightening because they bite but because of their sudden, quick movements. Darting about unpredictably, they seem to the phobic likely to jump out at him, to attack, however unlikely that possibility seems to everyone else and even to the phobic himself during more rational moments. Other common discrete phobias include those listed below. These are narrow fears that may have developed out of specific upsetting events. Like the simple animal phobias, they are common in childhood and usually fade with time. When present in adult life, however, they are likely to persist indefinitely unless treated.

1. Lightning and/or thunder
2. Darkness, as in a dark passageway or dark streets
3. Public speaking
4. Heights
5. The sight of blood
6. Swimming
7. Visiting a dentist

Most phobias, however, are not really the fear of a thing itself or of a particular set of circumstances, but rather the fear of the feelings that object or situation calls up in the affected person. Feeling trapped in an elevator, the phobic person becomes afraid that his panicky feelings will rise to such terrible proportions that he will have a heart attack or choke to death, or that he will lose control of himself, scream, or fall to the ground. He is afraid not only of what may happen to him but also of embarrassing himself by some outrageous show of behavior. Sometimes the condition becomes arrested at this point. If he is frightened only of elevators or closed-in places, he is said to be claustrophobic. If he avoids heights but can go anywhere else, he is called acrophobic. More commonly, however, the condition spreads. Since he can't run away from his own feelings, he is likely after a while to feel trapped anywhere—driving through a tunnel, sitting in a barbershop, waiting on line in a bank, or waiting any place where he feels he cannot, if he suddenly becomes desperate, leave immediately. If he is by himself anywhere, without immediate means of returning home, he feels stranded. So the phobia worsens. This complicated syndrome usually goes by the name agoraphobia.

Agoraphobia is defined by the latest *Diagnostic and Statistical Manual of Mental Disorders* as "a marked fear of being alone or being in public places from which escape might be difficult or help not available in case of sudden incapacitation." These few words do not adequately explain the variety of symptoms or convey the distress of the typical person who suffers from agoraphobia. A better understanding of the illness comes from considering representative cases: *

Janet was thirty-seven when she first came to the Phobia Clinic announcing with what seemed at first an odd enthusiasm that she was "an agoraphobic."

"It started when I was twenty-two," she said, sitting at the edge of her chair. "I was driving along in a car, and suddenly I had this awful feeling, like something terrible was going to happen. I thought it was my body at first. My heart started to pound a mile a minute. My mouth dried up. I couldn't catch my breath. I felt like I was going to have a heart attack or a fit. I was so shaky, I don't know how I got to the hospital without driving off the road and killing somebody. When I saw the doctor the next day, he told me there was nothing the matter with me. I was fine for about two weeks. Then one day I was sitting with my husband in a restaurant, and the same feeling came back, except worse. And for no reason. I felt dizzy too, like the floor was tilting. I couldn't swallow a thing, not even water. My mind was fuzzy. I thought I was going crazy. I had to leave before I lost control of myself and made a spectacle. This time the doctor did

---

* In order to preserve confidentiality, these cases and all others presented in this book are to some extent composites. As a further precaution, I have in every case substituted different names and changed all other identifying characteristics or circumstances.

all kinds of tests, but everything was normal. He gave me tranquilizers and told me to relax. It was okay for a week, but then the attacks started up again. I couldn't go in restaurants or drive far away from home. I felt trapped if I had to sit in church or the beauty parlor. After a while no place felt safe. I couldn't even visit my in-laws because how could I explain if I had to run away suddenly? Even in my house I began to have attacks. Somebody had to stay with me all the time in case I had to be taken to the hospital. I was anxious all the time, and sometimes I was sure that one minute more and I would go out of my mind."

According to Janet, her symptoms continued unabated for the next fourteen years except for a period of six months after the birth of her first child when inexplicably she was considerably improved. On two other occasions during brief vacations her symptoms vanished entirely, only to return later. During the course of her illness she had seen literally dozens of doctors, chiropractors, nutritionists, and other health-care practitioners, including a hypnotist. She had taken tranquilizers, antidepressants, antiarrythmic agents, vitamins, special diets, and had done special exercises including yoga. She was told to wear orthopedic shoes. None of these remedies helped. She had been subjected to stomach and bowel X rays, EEGs, EKGs, and an endocrine workup performed twice because the first examination gave a false positive result. On one occasion, because she complained so persistently of chest pain, she underwent coronary angiography. Why then, her interviewer asked, after she had undergone so many uninformative and unsuccessful treatments, was she in a good mood?

"Because after all these years I had gotten the idea I had some weird disease that the doctors never came across before. But yesterday I heard a lady on the radio telling all about her condition, which was exactly the same as mine. Now at least I know what's the matter with me. I've got agoraphobia!"

Theresa was phobic to some extent as far back as she could remember. She had been a clinging child and would cry for hours when left with a baby-sitter. It was weeks before she could adjust to being left alone in kindergarten. Concurrently, she developed a fear of dogs and other animals, especially snakes, to the point where she refused to walk in a park. These fears proved transient, however. She managed also in time to adjust well to school. She made friends readily, became a good student, and seemed to everyone a warm, responsive child. Even in these early years she gave evidence of an ability to draw well, a skill that became the basis in adult life for a successful career as a commercial artist. The only symptoms that troubled her to any extent while she was growing up were a vague sense of discomfort looking out the windows of tall buildings, an uneasiness when she traveled far from home, and, still, an embarrassing inability to stay by herself at home overnight. Another problem —perhaps more her mother's problem than hers—was a tendency to develop very minor physical complaints, serious enough in her mother's eyes to require a visit to a doctor's office and often to a series of doctors' offices.

In due course Theresa graduated college, married, and had a child. Except for being a "worrier," inclined especially to worry about her daughter's health as her mother had worried about hers, she was happy.

However, after a short illness at the age of twenty-seven, she developed occasional "anxiety attacks." These were moments when she felt shaky and distracted. Once she became so light-headed she had to lie down. These episodes recurred for many years at times when she was under special stress and at other times when there was no noticeable cause. She found tranquilizers helpful to some extent and always carried with her a number of pills and a vial of water so she could take them without a moment's delay. Certain places, such as church or the library, made her feel especially uncomfortable, as did large social gatherings such as weddings. She never attended funerals. She tolerated small family get-togethers by humming to herself and twisting a key chain tightly around a finger "like a lucky rabbit's foot." Despite these nagging limitations, she still thought of herself as happy. She would probably never have come for treatment had she not, again for no apparent reason, become depressed. She found herself then feeling anxious constantly rather than intermittently. She cried, particularly in the morning, and her sleep was interrupted by bad dreams. Eventually she showed a good response to antidepressant medication, including a general lessening of anxiety. She had fewer panic attacks, and her mood returned to normal.

At the age of thirty, Perry was the owner of a very successful electrical contracting business that he had begun only three years before. In every other aspect of his life he also seemed to be doing well. He was married and the father of a son. He had friends. He was regarded by everyone as unfailingly good-humored and capable. He had managed to keep secret from everyone except his wife his inability to drive more than one mile from his home. He was also unable to ride in elevators, a failing that he felt was ridiculous and that he kept even from her. Hiding these lifelong fears required complicated stratagems. He avoided most social engagements if they were beyond his safe perimeter by pretending to be ill or occupied urgently with business. If he had to go up high in an office building, he left time to walk up the stairs, and he made sure never to arrive in the company of anyone else. If he had been willing to explain to someone why he was afraid of elevators, he would not have known how to do so. He was vaguely concerned that the elevator might stop between floors, trapping him, but he knew that such a breakdown was unlikely and temporary in any case. Certainly he would be in no true danger. He had the foreboding, nevertheless, that were he trapped in an elevator even briefly, something awful would happen. He was especially afraid that he would vomit, although he had not vomited since he was a child.

Some time later, when Perry got the courage to speak to his older brother about his condition, his brother confided to him about *his* phobia: Over a period of fifteen years he had avoided crowds and speaking engagements because under those circumstances, he developed chest pains and palpitations. The two brothers listened sympathetically to each other's accounts, each thinking that the other's worries seemed farfetched and less threatening than his own.

Perry's symptoms remained stable over time. They neither worsened in severity nor spread to other areas. Nor did they improve except briefly on one notable occasion. One day Perry's son broke his arm in a bicycle accident. Without thinking of the possibility of vomiting and without any thought at all to his surroundings, he drove his son to a nearby hospital and later went with him up seven flights in an elevator to the operating suite. The following day, when the emergency was past, he was not able to return to the hospital.

Millie's phobia started abruptly at the age of twenty when she was attending a party. Suddenly and without apparent reason she felt panicky, dizzy, and unable to catch her breath. She began to tremble. She felt better only after leaving the party and returning home where she could lie down. Similar attacks recurred repeatedly, first only at parties or in classrooms, but after a while in any public place where she felt someone might notice that her hands were trembling. For that reason she found dealing with a bank teller or a cashier in a supermarket particularly trying and likely to cause her to retreat precipitously. Soon there were more and more places where she felt uncomfortable and sometimes overtly panicky and fewer places where she felt secure. She avoided all conveyances, including buses, trains, airplanes and, unless driven by her mother, automobiles. She avoided closed-in places such as elevators, tunnels, or windowless rooms; social situations from which she could not easily extricate herself, including parties, weddings, and family gatherings; situations of enforced passivity, such as waiting in line at a bank or supermarket, or a doctor's office. Finally, she was afraid of heights, especially bridges, train platforms, and the top floor of open-air garages. When she found herself unavoidably looking out from these high places, she was seized by the frightening impulse to jump. Like the panicky sensations that swept over her from time to time, it was a feeling she was not sure she could resist.

There came a time, finally, when she felt unsafe even in her own apartment. She could not shower because she imagined she would have to run out into the street or be taken away to the nearest hospital, and she didn't want to be embarrassed by being naked! She felt uneasy in her living room because of a large unshaded window which called to her mind the thought of jumping out. And she was afraid to be alone. Since she led such a constrained life, more limited certainly than that of most people who suffer from overt psychoses—presumably much more serious illnesses—it came as a surprise to the psychiatrist who visited her that within the security of her bedroom she appeared to be a warm, friendly, intellectually capable and adroit young woman. There was nothing about her manner to suggest that she was suffering any kind of emotional illness, let alone one so incapacitating.

Because the office of the nearest psychiatrist was over five miles from her home, Millie could not participate in out-patient psychotherapy. Consequently, she was admitted to a hospital. Treatment, however, which included major tranquilizers and antidepressants, produced only a minor and temporary improvement. Over the succeeding years she was readmitted a number of times and given many different tranquilizers, and on two occasions electric shock treatments, but with no better result. No medications blocked her panic attacks or calmed her to the extent that she could confront those situations that were frightening to her. Nevertheless she carried tranquilizers wherever she went and felt that she could not get through the day without them. Although Millie married and had children, her condition continued unchanged for the next twenty years. She wrote this letter to me:

"I have been agoraphobic for over thirty years. I have been to many doctors to no avail. In the beginning they kept telling me I was on the verge of a nervous breakdown and then gave me medicine, ups and downs, and everything, but they don't help; and I don't want to live on them the rest of my life anyway. I don't go anywhere. My car sits in the garage. If somehow I do go out with my husband, I have an attack. He is very patient, but even he is coming to his wits' end. My biggest symptoms are hyperventilation, shaking, dry mouth, a light-headed feeling, and I can't swallow. I have terrible palpitation attacks. It scares the hell out of me, and I don't want anyone to see me have an attack. I feel so totally isolated and am becoming more and more depressed every day. I don't know where to turn for help. I feel that if I don't get help soon, something terrible will happen, whatever that "something" is. My youngest daughter, who is fifteen, is developing some phobic-type symptoms, and it worries me. I know she's learning this fear from me. I not only ruined my life, but now I'm ruining hers. I feel so guilty because I can't set a good example for her. I feel like half a person. Isn't there something to help someone like me?"

These, then, are the varied presentations of agoraphobia. In this severe form it may affect 2 to 3 percent of the population. Since for one reason or another phobics may not present themselves for treatment, no one can know for sure. If those who are less severely ill are counted (someone who is not fearful in general, indeed, who does not think of himself as phobic but who, nevertheless, refuses to fly, or avoids driving on highways or looking out high windows, or is uncomfortable sitting in a windowless room or a theater balcony), the number would rise dramatically. *These lesser phobias are all variants of agoraphobia since they represent not the fear of a particular thing—such as the "specific" phobias listed previously—but the fear of specific feelings that arise in certain situations.* Consequently, such phobias tend to spread. Although someone occasionally manages to go through life with a phobia limited, for example, to escalators, more typically such a person will also come to be afraid of heights, perhaps, or of riding in the back seat of a car. He might then be said to be suffering from two or three separate phobias, but his illness has more in common with a full-blown agoraphobia than with the specific phobias. The treatment for such a person is the same as for a more generalized agoraphobia. In short, there are some people who are only mildly affected by agoraphobia and for only a limited time while others suffer a lifelong disabling condition. Some have only a few fears, and these seem to be only an exaggeration of those that beset most people—the fear of being ill, being left alone, or being helpless. Others, however, seem to be afraid of everything. But always present in the illness, as it manifests itself differently in these different people, are certain cardinal symptoms. These are the elements that characterize an agoraphobia:

1. *A pervasive feeling of anxiety, rising at times to the level of panic.* The panic itself may be experienced physically as a crescendo of symptoms suggesting a heart attack,

a seizure of some sort, or even impending death. Among these physical symptoms are the following:

a. Dizziness, more an unsteadiness than a true vertigo: There is a sense of the floor tilting rather than the room going around.

b. Shortness of breath: The phobic may have a sense of being unable to catch his breath and consequently hyperventilates.*

c. Palpitations: The phobic becomes aware of his heartbeat, which may seem to him to be quickened or irregular.

d. Chest pain: The reasons why anxious people have chest pain are many. Someone who is emotionally tense may hold his chest muscles rigidly, causing pain very much in the way a different person might suffer tension headaches or low back pain. Most commonly, however, chest pain in anxious people is attributable to motility disturbances in the gastro-intestinal tract. Spasm of a muscular valve of the stomach, besides causing heartburn, can cause severe pain radiating into the left arm. Such pain need not, therefore, indicate a heart attack.

e. Weakness and trembling: For similar reasons anxious people tense the muscles in their arms and legs.

---

* The hyperventilation syndrome is a common but striking accompaniment of anxiety states. The anxious person has the subjective sensation of being unable to catch his breath, although in fact he breathes perfectly well. Actually he is overbreathing. As he puffs and sighs, he breathes off an excess of carbon dioxide, altering the acid-base balance of the blood—which affects other elements in the blood to produce a clinical state resembling tetany. The affected person feels light-headed and dizzy. His fingertips and lips may begin to tingle. Usually this uncomfortable state proceeds no further, but it can last many minutes and intermittently for hours.

Breathing in and out of a paper bag is frequently prescribed for hyperventilation. The carbon dioxide that has been exhaled in excess is then breathed in again. But it is a remedy that exaggerates the significance of the symptom to the patient and also makes him feel foolish. If he is reassured and left alone, the condition subsides by itself.

After prolonged exertion these muscles feel weak and tremble. Sometimes they hurt.

   f. Pallor or, conversely, flushing.

In addition to these symptoms, so striking they themselves become frightening, the panicky person can suffer all those varied complaints one commonly associates with being nervous: dry mouth; trouble swallowing; cold, sweaty palms; headache; blurry vision; a sense of seeing things out of focus; ringing in the ears; cramps; nausea; frequent urination; diarrhea; and so on. Almost any physical sensation can grow out of anxiety; in turn, any physical symptom can further worry the phobic, who becomes concerned that he is suffering from a serious, underlying physical disorder. Experiencing palpitations, the phobic may become afraid that he is having a heart attack. A feeling of nausea may lead him to think he has an ulcer. Even if he understands these symptoms to be caused psychologically, he may think that they will nevertheless by themselves bring on a physical illness. Although he is continually reassured by his physician and his family that he is not sick and is not becoming sick, he continues to be afraid.

Alternately, the panic attack may be experienced as primarily emotional, a sense of spiraling fear that threatens loss of control and helplessness. The panicky person suddenly feels that he is likely to fall to the ground in a faint or scream or act recklessly, perhaps violently. If he is driving a car, it may seem to him he is on the verge of driving off the road, and the danger seems worse moment by moment. Someone else, more commonly a woman, may be anguished by the thought that she will rip off her clothes publicly or commit some other act equally embarrassing. *There is no comfort in the fact that previous panic attacks which were just as severe never did cause any such emotional or physical calamity.* It always seems to the panicky person that he was saved only at the last minute by escaping. This time—or the next time—there may not be time to escape. Consequently, each time that he becomes panicky he has the powerful urge to withdraw from whatever place he happens to be. Subsequently, he is likely to avoid returning to that place or any place like it, in anticipation that if he does, he will once again be overcome by such feelings. Someone may start off avoiding a particular stretch of highway where he first experienced a panic attack, then all highways, then quite possibly all roads. Soon there are more and more places to avoid and fewer places where he can feel safe and comfortable. Usually the farther away from home he is, the worse he feels. The horizons of his life shrink inexorably from the world at large to a particular city, then to a particular neighborhood. Ultimately, he may feel anxious everywhere except in his own house, sometimes in his own room. He may explain his wish to stay at home by claiming that the highways are too dangerous to drive on or that his neighborhood is too dangerous to walk through, but he knows really that those fears are exaggerated. Even if these dangers were real, they would be poor reason to hide away from the world. Perversely, sometimes home itself is no haven. Unless another person is present or immediately available, he may still feel trapped. Even there he is beset by fears, most of which he recognizes as irrational. He is anxious to some extent everywhere. It is the pattern of avoidance that determines the phobia.

2. *The pattern of phobic avoidance.* There are many different situations for which people are phobic, but these overlap and merge into one another and are usually multiple in any particular individual. Someone phobic, therefore, typically avoids a number of different places. Because phobics tend to feel trapped in the same circumstances, the pattern of avoidance is remarkably the same from one phobic to the next. Frightening situations include closed-in spaces such as elevators, tunnels, buses, trains, airplanes, and other conveyances; heights, such as bridges, escalators, and subway platforms; and wide-open areas such as beaches and stadiums. The list of social circumstances that are intoler-

able include public places such as department stores, restaurants and, especially, quiet places such as churches, libraries, and theaters. The phobic may not be able to wait on line at banks or bus stops. Ordinary conversation may seem to him a trap because it will prevent him from leaving abruptly. He may not be able to attend family functions, particularly if they are large, formal affairs. Most important, he may not be able to work.

The course of the illness is somewhat less characteristic. Some phobics can date their fears back to their earliest memories. An exaggerated difficulty of going off to kindergarten sometimes merges into a full-blown school phobia, which is really an early version of an agoraphobia. More often the condition seems to appear for the first time in adolescence, occasionally later, sometimes considerably later in life. It may suddenly appear in the context of an unpleasant event that stimulates unconscious fantasies, or it may develop insidiously. Most typically it comes abruptly, without obvious reason. Even in these cases there is often a history of childhood fears. These may be varied—a school or animal phobia, a fear of the dark or of being left alone. Whenever the illness starts, it almost always does so dramatically with a panic attack. Sometimes soon after, sometimes only over a period of years, a pattern emerges of intermittent panic attacks occurring in a growing variety of places, and the avoidance of all those places in an attempt to prevent such attacks. Just as the condition comes on without apparent reason, it may go away again, only to return months or years later. More commonly, however, once a severe phobia has developed, it tends without treatment to persist indefinitely, not infrequently over the course of a lifetime.

Depression occurs along the way so frequently that it may be considered a part of the illness. It takes two forms: First, the natural discouragement, sometimes despair, that comes from enduring such a persistently limited and uncomfortable life, and second, the endogenous depression, so-called because it seems to erupt without any external cause.* Depression is important because it frequently causes agitation indistinguishable from a panic attack. By so doing it may initiate the process described above that leads eventually to a severe phobia. To some extent the beneficial effect antidepressant drugs are said to have in the treatment of agoraphobia may be attributable to the overlap between these two conditions. Finally, the misdiagnosis of hypoglycemia, food allergies or sensitivities, and vitamin deficiencies is such a common occurrence during the course of an agoraphobia that it should be considered a complication of the illness. Struck by the pronounced physical aspects of the panic attack, the phobic goes from one doctor to another until he falls into the hands of "specialists" who make these diagnoses on everyone who comes into their offices. As a consequence, the phobic, whose life is seriously restricted to begin with, becomes further handicapped by adhering to peculiar diets and other arbitrary limitations on his daily life.

The Causes

An agoraphobe is typically a child of parents who are themselves, one or both of them, phobic to some degree.† That this condition runs in families is well-known, and given in evidence sometimes that there is an underlying genetic—physiological, that is—vulnerability to the illness. It may be so. Some children are born more sensitive than others. A loud noise makes one baby jump and cry while another moves about vaguely for a moment, then subsides again into sleep. Certain inborn qualities of reac-

* See chapter on special conditions associated with agoraphobia.

† In response to a questionnaire sent to all the phobics who communicated to the White Plains Hospital Phobia Clinic, over half replied that they had a parent who was unequivocally phobic, impeded to a significant extent in the management of his or her life.

tivity tend to persist throughout life and so form the underpinnings of personality. But if one child is more vulnerable than another, more likely perhaps to be subject somehow to a panic attack, that would scarcely explain the complicated syndrome that is agoraphobia. There are some people who experience panic attacks repeatedly without ever becoming phobic. In my opinion, the familial occurrence of agoraphobia is accounted for more readily in terms of the contagion of ideas than by an obscure physical predilection.

The parents of phobics, even when they are not themselves explicitly phobic, are to some extent frightened people—although they don't often think of themselves that way. Their fears may be expressed only as exaggerations of commonly held beliefs. They worry about the danger of traveling on subways or walking through the streets at night, or about the danger to their child when he plays with another child who has been sick or when he goes out in cold weather without wearing a scarf or when he rides a bicycle through city streets, and so on. Parents communicate a frightened feeling to their children when they voice such concerns over and over. After a while the children see the world as a threatening place. Even their own feelings, especially their aggressive and sexual impulses, may seem frightening to them; consequently, they grow to be in conflict about asserting themselves. The fears that an agoraphobe carries into adulthood may also seem to be many, but they are really two:

He is afraid of losing control of his feelings. The panic attack itself represents the welling up of unconscious feelings, often anger. Such a person may be afraid of driving a car because of the fear of driving into people. Or, if he has an urge to hurt himself, unconscious though it may be, he avoids open windows or other dangerous places—subway platforms, for instance, or bridges—where he may become conscious of the temptation to jump. The self-consciousness that is so characteristic of the phobic may represent paradoxically the wish to deal with exhibitionistic feelings. The phobic is always oblivious to these underlying, unconscious ideas. Treatment may proceed successfully without his becoming aware of or being made to acknowledge such urges, if they do, in fact, exist. But it should be kept in mind that the panic attack represents at least the sense of losing control. It is an idea expressed most powerfully as the fear of screaming or going crazy.

The second fear the phobic suffers is of being helpless, a thought that may present itself to his mind transformed as a fear of being trapped, for instance, in an elevator or an airplane, or at a barbershop, or waiting on line at a bus stop. Any situation from which he cannot immediately escape is intolerable.

These fears, which develop at first in specific situations, invade more and more areas of life until there is no place that is secure. Finally, different fears coalesce into the fear of being overwhelmed by panic. It is the fear of fear itself.

One psychodynamic formulation of the cause of agoraphobia runs as follows: The agoraphobe has an ambivalent relationship with his, or more commonly her, mother, who is usually overprotective. In order to become independent he must assert himself in ways that seem to him to be hostile to his mother. Doing so makes him feel guilty, and consequently, paradoxically, he draws even closer to his mother in order to feel secure. He may wish to remain home from school in order to make sure his mother is "all right." Long after everyone else has grown away from his parents, the phobic still needs his mother—and as a result often comes to resent her. But he cannot break away. The phobia, sometimes expressed directly by the phobic needing his mother literally within reach, is the outcome of that dependent relationship. So the story goes, and certainly this account describes many phobics. Many others it does not. What can be said for certain, however, is that somehow, along the way of growing up, the phobic has developed certain misconceptions about himself and about the world. These mistaken ideas, described below, form the basis of the illness:

1. Although the phobic may not say so explicitly, he regards the world as fundamentally a dangerous place. For someone inclined to this idea, there seems to be plenty of corroborating evidence in the daily newspaper. Planes crash. Trains slide off embankments. Buildings burn down. Cars run into each other, sometimes seven or eight at a time. If these catastrophes seem somewhat removed, there is always the report from a neighbor of someone mugged or raped on a nearby street. Such things really happen, but the phobic, anxious in general, takes closer note of these incidents than other people do and exaggerates their frequency and significance. If it is natural for most people to worry when their children stay out late, phobics worry more, even when their children are older and the hour is not so late. Since they express the reasonable concerns of ordinary people, it is difficult to convince them that the degree to which they worry is unreasonable. These preoccupations often predate the onset of the phobia itself and frequently date back to childhood when their parents expressed similar concerns. Specific phobias grow out of these general fears. For example, when a parent says, "Call me when you arrive so I know you got there safely," he communicates the message that the child (who may be thirty years old) *may not* arrive safely. It is no wonder that someone responding to such remarks all through his growing up might someday develop an airplane phobia. Similarly, comments such as "Don't take the car, it's raining," "Don't take the car, it's dark out," "Don't take the car, there'll be traffic," "Don't take the car there, it's a bad neighborhood," "Don't take the car, it's too long a ride," add up to, "Don't take the car, driving is dangerous." It's a short step from this idea to a full-blown driving phobia.

These commonplace sentiments, when repeated over and over, reflect an attitude, a heightened awareness of danger, which is both an accompaniment and a cause of phobic states and which is communicated from one generation to the next.

2. The phobic person considers physical health to be a precarious matter, as if the human body were a delicate machine not quite up to the varied challenge of day-to-day living. Once again, this idea is learned in childhood. It characterizes the phobic's point of view even prior to the onset of the phobia itself, and it is likely to be passed on by the phobic to his or her children. And, again, it is only an exaggeration of views commonly expressed by others:

"Don't go out in the rain, you'll get sick."

"Stay out of the sun, you'll get sick."

"Take your rubbers off in the house or you'll catch a cold."

"You have a cold, so you'd better take it easy or you'll get pneumonia."

"If you don't eat a good breakfast, you'll get sick."

"Don't go swimming after lunch, you'll get a cramp."

"Don't watch television so much, it's bad for your eyes."

"Don't crack your knuckles, you'll get arthritis."

"Don't eat so fast, you'll get nauseous."

"Don't drink cold water when you're overheated, it's bad for you."

"You have to get eight hours of sleep at your age."

"Don't go out now, it's over ninety degrees."

"You worked all day, now rest."

And so on.

Any deviation from normal physical routine is seen as dangerous. Going without sleep for a night or skipping a meal or exercising strenuously *is seen as unhealthy;* and such ideas are so ingrained, they seem reasonable! It is not surprising, then, that the phobic is sensitive to any unusual physical sensation. The normal physiological responses to stress or excitement—a quickened heart beat, deeper respiration, tense muscles—are cause for concern because they are considered harbingers of an impending physical breakdown. With that in mind, the phobic hurries off to see a doctor. Often, in order to allay his patient's anxiety, the physician goes through the motions of a medical workup, not realizing that he too is communicating a message: "It may turn out your tests are negative this time and you are not suffering from a medical illness, *but your symptoms are such that I think a physical illness is possible.*" The next time the phobic experiences a strange bodily sensation—likely to feel just a little different than the last time—he returns to the doctor convinced that this time he really is ill. Besides, he asks himself and his doctor, how long can the body stand up to the repeated onslaughts of panic attacks? The phobic believes that the fear of a heart attack, along with all the natural bodily reactions to fear, can actually cause the heart attack. Along with this general readiness to worry about his health—and, for that matter, the health of everyone else who matters to him—he is likely to have specific fears of heart disease or cancer.

The following misconceptions, central to the phobic process, grow out of the first two.

3. Although the phobic is anxious in general, he is preoccupied principally by the fear of becoming panicky. It is probably this fear rather than the panic itself that causes him to avoid and withdraw from certain situations. That concern is founded in turn on certain misconceptions about the panicky feeling itself:

a. that it will get worse and worse every moment until the affected person loses control and behaves irrationally, recklessly, or in an embarrasing way;

b. that it will cause a physical breakdown of some sort, usually choking or a heart attack;

c. that it will incapacitate the affected person so that he is unable to drive, speak publicly, write his name without visibly shaking, or even walk;

d. that it will not terminate by itself or by any effort of the phobic person short of escaping from the situation;

e. that evidence of the feeling is written all over the phobic's face and in other aspects of his behavior, so that the fact of his panic is visible to everyone;

f. that it may worsen *beyond a point of no return*, so that remaining in the phobic situation one more moment would be too much. The sense of spiraling fear is thought to reflect a real spiraling of danger.

The fact that none of these things has ever happened in the past, although the phobic person may have experienced numerous panic attacks, is attributed to accident, to leaving the situation just in the nick of time, to the chance arrival of a spouse or some other trusted person, to the coincidence of some event that served to distract. And so on.

4. Time and distance stretch out peculiarly for the phobic so that very short periods of time seem very long, very short distances seem great, and great distances and long periods of time seem to be off the face of the earth and forever. Traffic lights seem truly to stay red for four or five minutes, as may a ride in an elevator. A phobic may sit relatively comfortably at the rear of an auditorium or church, or in an aisle seat, but be unable to sit farther in or farther down. That insignificant difference—the extra few feet and the extra second or two it would take to leave—is the difference between feeling safe and feeling trapped. After a while a perimeter may develop—the edge of town, the boundaries of the neighborhood, the block on which the phobic lives, or even his apartment—outside of which it is not possible to go. It is as if the end of the world came at the edge of a particular intersection. To go farther would be to risk getting lost irretrievably. To be by oneself in an apartment with family living across town and a wife or husband at the other end of a telephone is to feel nevertheless hopelessly alone.

5. The phobic regards his condition as shameful and embarrassing, and thinks everyone else will also consider it so. Sometimes unable to do ordinary things children can

do, he feels ridiculous. Consequently, he becomes self-conscious. He invests a tremendous effort in trying to hide his nervousness, endlessly giving excuses for avoiding social occasions, work, or vacations. In the end, living such a secret and circumscribed life, he becomes depressed.

6. Finally, the phobic comes to believe that he has a condition unknown to doctors, progressive and incurable. He may believe, for instance, that he has an obscure physical illness or a beginning psychosis. Most important, *he believes it is a condition over which he has no control.*

In all of these ideas, the phobic is in error. The world is not, for the most part, a dangerous place. The reason why crime and catastrophe appear continuously in the news is precisely that they are still unusual enough to be newsworthy. Similarly, most people are healthy throughout most of their lives. Despite occasional random pains and peculiar sensations, people manage. The human body has evolved over millions of years to survive the routine stresses, both physical and psychological, to which it is subject. Accident and illness do occur, of course, and to some extent they are preventable. However, all of life should not be given over to warding off danger, most of which is imaginary. Human beings are able to maintain themselves very well despite occasional lapses of diet or disturbances of routine, including sleep. They thrive in every climate, exposed to every variation of circumstance and stress, including psychological stress. *As a rule, the body does not tend to break down.* Psychological responses to fear, for example, are short-lived and do not in themselves weaken the body.

The phobic's misconceptions about time and distance are seen, even by the phobic, as somehow in error. But what is recognized intellectually on the conscious level as false still seems true on an emotional level. The phobic feels trapped, lost, or beyond help when actually he is in control of his circumstances. And perfectly safe.

Neither is the phobic correct about his attitude toward the condition itself. When he is finally persuaded to speak openly to people about his phobia, their response is likely to be much more understanding than he had expected. Perhaps one-third of those people will react to the news with "ho hum" or the equivalent. The varied symptoms of a phobia seem unremarkable and not terribly interesting. A surprisingly high number of people, perhaps another third, will respond enthusiastically by announcing that they have, or have had, similar fears—or one of their friends did, or one of their relatives. Phobias, in mild form at least, are common. Finally, another quarter of this group to whom the phobic allows himself to confide react with interest. They ask questions about the phobia and may enter into a conversation of some length about the subject. They are not so impressed as a rule, however, that they are likely to remember from one day to the next that there are certain situations that make the phobic uncomfortable. Phobias do not seem so extraordinary to them, and certainly not so shameful or noteworthy as to be memorable. *The illness does not suggest weakness to them* or to the others to whom the phobic confides. There is, finally, a small number of confidants who react unsympathetically, either with a sneer—"Ah, c'mon, you could drive up here if you really wanted to"—or with contempt—"You mean you can't even go into an elevator?" Invariably these are people who tend to look down on everybody anyway for imaginary failings if they can't find anything real to deprecate. Their good opinion can't be earned and isn't worth having.

The phobic is also wrong about the panic attack:

1. It does not cause a physical derangement or psychosis. Schizophrenia and other such serious illnesses do not grow out of panic states.

2. It does not get worse and worse. The psychological effect is similar to watching a spiral drawn on a piece of paper

as the paper is turned. There is an illusion of spinning but no real change. The sensation of panic is sensed subjectively as a spiraling, ever-worsening fear, but there is no objective evidence of actual change. At its most extreme the panic usually lasts only a minute or two, then diminishes, although sometimes only to rise again a few minutes later. This sequence repeated a number of times, as may happen, can give the mistaken impression of an ever-increasing, spiraling fear. Similarly, panic by itself does not cause someone to faint,* scream, or behave foolishly. Or run away. Or lose control. The phobic characteristically maintains such tight control, it is not usually possible to tell when he is having a panic attack! †

Most important of all, the phobic is wrong in regarding his condition as incurable.

These various misconceptions that underlie agoraphobia are learned over a period of years, sometimes over the course of a lifetime. They are not learned casually, as one learns in a classroom. They represent basic attitudes toward life and an inclination to behave in certain ways, and they are consequently part of the bedrock of personality. They are learned mostly at home. And they cannot be unlearned in a classroom. A psychiatrist's assurances carry little weight set against parental warnings offered repeatedly during the formative years. The phobic must learn what he needs to know—how to be unafraid—by entering into the phobic situation itself. Treatment consists in facilitating that learning process.

---

* Fainting *can* occur in a very small group of phobics whose fears are predominantly of blood, injury, or medical procedures. Confronting these threatening circumstances, they may develop "vasovagal syncope." At those times, however, they are not, strictly speaking, in a panic attack. Their condition too resolves with the graduated exposure program recommended in this book.

† Those who know the phobic person well may be able to see past this facade. Sometimes a spouse or a close friend will ask, "What's the matter with you? You look pale (or flushed)." Most of the time what is being commented on is not truly a change of color but a change of expression. Someone who is customarily smiling and talkative may seem ill if he suddenly falls silent and seems distracted.

Character and Motivation

The phobic is often berated—sometimes by people who ought to know better, such as family, friends, or even physicians—for being "unmotivated" or "dependent." The term "dependent" calls up an image of a weak, indecisive person clinging to everyone, incapable of making plans or of running a business or a family, or in other ways arranging his or her life. Certainly phobics tend to cling, literally, to a trusted person when they feel panicky, and there are some who fit this stereotype exactly. But by far the larger number are adroit, competent people who relate well to others and manage their daily lives sensibly and with sensitivity. They are as diverse as human beings in general. But if any generalization can be made about them, it would be drawn in positive terms. Phobics tend as a group to be warm, friendly, reliable, and responsive (sometimes too much so) to the feelings of others. They seem invariably to have a good sense of humor. More than a few are artists. Most of the men are financially successful. A surprising number own their own businesses. Often they show initiative, even courage. Limited in many ways, severe phobics may still retain the ability to enjoy themselves. They need not be either passive or dependent.

Nor are they unmotivated to get well.

"If you really wanted to get treatment, you would be able to come to my office," some psychiatrists say.

Nonsense.

"If you were truly interested in getting an education, you would manage somehow to stay in my classroom," certain teachers declare smugly.

More nonsense.

A family member might insist, "You could come to my wedding, if you really cared."

Baloney!

Phobics have no less inclination to be well, to learn, and

to have fun than anyone else. They just don't know how in the face of their phobia to manage these tasks. More specifically, they don't know *how* to get past these varied and discrete obstacles:

1. Planning to venture into threatening situations;
2. Coping with the awful anticipation of failure and of public disgrace;
3. Enlisting the help of others who are sympathetic;
4. Dealing with the unpredictable behavior of others;
5. Finding alternatives to running away.

And so on.

There are those who find so little in life appealing that they are unwilling to put up with the painful and prolonged business of getting well; they would just as soon stay home. But they are rare exceptions. The great majority of phobics wish to participate actively in life. They aggressively and courageously pursue any treatment program that will allow them to do so—just as long as they understand precisely what that program requires of them. In the following pages such a program is described.

Chapter 2

TREATMENT

Since agoraphobia grows out of certain misconceptions about the world, treatment is a process of education. There are two learning experiences essential to the complete recovery from agoraphobia:

1. The phobic must learn—a little at a time—that he can tolerate the phobic situation. If he is afraid of elevators, he can begin by looking at elevators—simply watching them come and go—then briefly standing in one, then going a single floor accompanied by a helper or a friend, then remaining alone in a moving elevator for perhaps only ten or twenty seconds, then for minutes until in the end he feels comfortable in elevators, in any elevator. Similarly, someone phobic of department stores must slowly get used to shopping and remaining alone in that situation. Even a bridge can be crossed in such a way—a little bit at a time. A success in one phobic situation makes coping in other places easier. If one dangerous place seems less frightening, so do all the others. The perimeter within which the phobic can live comfortably begins to expand, just as it had shrunk in the past when the condition was worsening. This process by which the phobic learns to be unafraid, although difficult, is straightforward. The more time the individual stays in the phobic situation, the less frightening that situation becomes.

All during this process, so simple in principle, are many difficulties that must be confronted one at a time. It is with the intention of helping the reader overcome these day-to-day obstacles that this book has been written. Other people have traveled this path successfully. Their experience, and the experience of those who were less successful, has made it possible to know which treatment devices work and which do not.

2. Much more difficult, the phobic must learn to tolerate the feeling of panic itself! It may seem that the very term "panic" suggests an overwhelming and uncontrollable feeling, but the fact is that with practice and training one can distance oneself from the feeling and even learn how to turn it off. Although a considerable number of exposures may be required, someone who experiences this terrible feeling over and over again comes to understand eventually that it is not in itself injurious and sooner or later—usually sooner—every panic attack goes away. Still, the typical phobic has suffered panic attacks very many times in the past without getting used to the feeling and without coming to believe any such thing. Why should these new trials lead to a different result? The difference lies in the attitude with which the phobic person comes to that experience. Intent only on leaving the frightening situation as quickly as possible, he pays no real attention to what is actually happening to him. When he approaches the phobic situation purposely, however, with the willingness and even the *intention* of becoming panicky, his psychological set allows him to master his feelings. It is a fundamentally different experience. Under such circumstances, it is sometimes difficult to have a panic attack! The expectation of the phobic colors his emotional reactions. The essential difference is, perhaps, as it is in other aspects of phobic behavior, between being active and being passive. It is the act of making something happen rather than waiting for something to happen. The phobic comes to regard the panic attack as an opportunity to practice different coping techniques,

and not as a premonitory sign of disaster. At the end of treatment the phobic person usually continues to have occasional panic attacks—short-lived and at increasing intervals—but they seem to him then simply a very unpleasant feeling with no more significance than a sudden stomachache—certainly no reason to discontinue whatever he is doing and leave immediately for home.

It is easy to speak glibly about the process of learning, but it should be understood from the start that the improvement of agoraphobia that usually comes with exposure therapy *does not come easily or quickly*. Learning takes place only in the phobic situation and comes only with practice. There are ten principles to keep in mind.

Ten Principles of Exposure Therapy

1. *Know the condition*—its usual symptoms and its usual course. The phobic must know, in particular, exactly how the condition affects him.

Most phobics begin treatment thinking they know only too well how their illness affects them, but the fact is they are so obsessed by the sense of danger that they pay no attention to anything else. They should come to know what thoughts or circumstances set off the panic, how often those same thoughts and circumstances fail to cause a panic attack, how long the panic lasts, what sort of actions lessen or turn off the panic, and so on. This information will prove useful in devising coping strategies. They must learn how much they can do on any particular day without feeling exhausted and how much they can do on days they think they can't do anything. They must learn from observing themselves—and also from this account—what to expect stage by stage, sometimes minute by minute, when they go to a party or a movie theater for the first time, or decide for the first time to take a plane trip. *Most important, they have to know what to expect all during the process of recov-*

ery. Getting better is not an uninterrupted improvement day by day. Some days the phobic cannot do what he managed readily the day before. The day after that, for no obvious reason, he may be able to accomplish much more. Even at the end of a successful treatment, the phobic has no guarantee that he will never become panicky again. Getting better certainly does not mean he will never become anxious again. It means that he will become unafraid of such feelings even when on occasion they do recur, and it means he will no longer consider avoiding any place or set of circumstances simply because he fears his own emotional reaction. Someone who is aggressive and steadfast and who cooperates fully in treatment, practicing every day, will *still* be troubled by symptoms for a considerable period of time.

Millie, the patient I described earlier, began treatment anew. The psychiatrist she saw was willing, the first few times they met, to come to her house. During these sessions he was able to convince her that he understood exactly what she was experiencing and was optimistic nevertheless about their ability to overcome her problem if they worked together. With some difficulty, finally, he obtained a measure of her trust. Then they set out together, slowly, to leave her house. The first panic attack she experienced in his presence took place a few feet outside her front door. With him there, though—a doctor, after all—she felt a little safer. If she was going to have a heart attack or faint or whatever, he would know what to do. They talked for a while, long enough for her panic to subside a little, then they walked a few steps farther before turning back. The next time they went out together, she was able shakily to reach the end of her street before turning back. This time she had no panic attack.

In such a way they proceeded from one street to the next. Sometimes Millie suffered one or two panic attacks and then seemed to be anxious all the rest of the day; other times her progress seemed to be effortless or at least painless. It was weeks before she felt comfortable, however, in her immediate neighborhood. But then after one more week of work she was able to go anywhere in town, often by herself. She was still panicky from time to time, and over a particular stretch of a few days she seemed to be panicky more than ever, but by then she realized that these terrible feelings never lasted more than a minute and a half! She tried frantically during these brief episodes to distract herself by talking to people or writing in a diary that she always carried with her; but on more than one occasion she found herself overcome by her fear and running—literally running—home. But the next day she was back at that frightening place.

In a similar step-by-step fashion she introduced herself into social situations—small family gatherings and, after a while, parties. She found these tasks more difficult, especially during the weeks following an attack of the flu. It seemed as if having to remain home in bed made it harder afterward to reenter phobic situations, even those she thought she had already conquered. Still, she persevered and discovered a few months later that in many places where she could not have gone previously she now felt entirely comfortable. She began driving again and within a year was working—at two jobs! With some trepidation but, it turned out, with no difficulty she took her first plane flight. During the next two years she no longer felt constrained in any way. Her phobia was gone entirely. Still, for reasons that never became clear, at distant intervals the panicky feelings returned—very briefly.

This course is typical in a number of respects:

a. Progress was not consistent. Although Millie did well, there were times when she did indeed fail and withdraw from the phobic situation.

b. Panic attacks came more frequently during initial encounters with the phobic situation. Yet, even when Millie was plainly improving, there was a time when she was suffering panic attacks more frequently than prior to treatment.

c. Often when Millie anticipated becoming panicky, she was not anxious at all. There came a time in treatment when sometimes the anticipation of entering the phobic situation was worse than actually being in that situation.

d. As time went on, there were more and more areas in which Millie could function comfortably; but still she suffered occasional panic attacks, even at times and places where she usually felt safe.

e. Even after the phobic is "cured," he may be panicky on rare occasions, briefly, and such was the case with Millie. Her reaction to being panicky, however, had changed. It was simply a feeling, however unpleasant, that she knew would leave her a moment or two later.

Such is the course of a successful treatment. It is not reasonable to expect faster progress. Someone proceeding even at a slower pace can still be cured entirely and should not become discouraged.

2. *Enter into the phobic situation.* This is always a painful process but bearable when managed properly. Without entering into the phobic situation, no progress is possible.

The phobic begins by constructing a hierarchy of uncomfortable or frightening situations, ranging from those circumstances that are tolerable, although somewhat difficult, to those that he currently finds impossible to confront. Then, systematically, he enters into these situations, beginning with the easiest. In time, as these places become more tolerable—which they do—he confronts those that are more difficult. Some things that initially seem as if they will be forever beyond reach become doable in the end. So much is easy to say, of course, and hard to accomplish. Certain rules must be kept in mind:

a. It is helpful to plan ahead of time, taking into consideration what is likely to happen—even the very worst the phobic can imagine—and planning what to do in that event to make the situation more manageable. To some extent it is possible to "desensitize" in fantasy. This is called cognitive rehearsal. Sometimes the plan should include the possibility of a temporary "escape."

When Millie committed herself to attend a family wedding reception, which took place on the fifth floor of a downtown hotel, it became necessary to plan ahead of time how she was going to do it. A few of the matters she and her psychiatrist discussed were:

i. the route to the hotel, the possibility of getting stuck in traffic, and the opportunities for turning back briefly if that became necessary;

ii. what explanation of her worries she should give to her cousin who was going to drive her;

iii. how to avoid a crowded elevator, what to do on the elevator to make herself feel more comfortable, and how to handle the unlikely possibility of getting stuck in the elevator;

iv. the uncomfortable moment when she would walk into a ballroom full of people whom she hadn't seen for a long time, and what to say if someone noticed her hands shaking;

v. the appropriateness of leaving the reception abruptly if she became panicky, and how to escape for a few minutes and still be able to return.

Most important, Millie had to know ahead of time what she was likely to feel during the few days before the party when she was anticipating the worst, at that moment later on when the elevator doors opened in front of her, and at that especially awful moment when she would have to dance.

Of course, it is not possible to predict such things with accuracy, but the *range* of possible reactions is known and can be anticipated. Along the way of preparing, the phobic who feels trapped everywhere comes to understand he is not really trapped anywhere.

b. It is better to start with the intention of entering a phobic situation *and turn back* at the last moment (or even long before the last moment) than not to start at all. This is not a philosophical argument about the way to approach life (although it would not be a bad philosophy). It is a plain observation that difficult phobic tasks seem less difficult from close up. Often what seems undoable or unthinkable from afar can be managed relatively easily when someone stands on the threshold of that task. Merely coming repeatedly to that threshold makes crossing over finally possible. A man afraid to board a bus may find that his level of anxiety has decreased *simply by standing for a considerable period of time at a bus stop*, watching passengers embark and disembark. A woman who has managed to get as far as a subway platform is likely to discover on a subsequent occasion that she can actually board the train. Starting helps. Sometimes even getting ready to start is a useful first step.

c. The speed with which the phobic proceeds up the hierarchy he has constructed does not matter to his eventual recovery. Small initial steps require as much effort—and are as important—as larger steps later on. For example, a housebound woman may in a certain period of time and by dint of a certain effort manage to get a few feet down her front walk to the mailbox, remaining for a minute or two before hurrying home. The same effort put in later on may enable her to walk a block and a half away from home. Still later, the same additional effort may carry her five blocks, and later on an additional mile. With therapy the perimeter that encloses the phobic expands in geometric progression. *The first few steps are as hard to take as the last hundred miles.*

d. Any "crutch" that makes those first few steps easier is acceptable. A suitable "crutch" might be the company of a sympathetic friend, a crossword puzzle to distract oneself, or even medication. Like a real crutch, these devices serve a real purpose, even though there comes a time as treatment progresses when, like a crutch, they can be discarded.

e. It is important to devise a daily plan ahead of time for engaging in phobic tasks, and a serious attempt should be made to stick to it. One should not be deterred by a tired feeling, a depressed feeling, or a sick feeling. Or by cloudy or rainy weather, or by a busy schedule, or by some unexpected obligation. It is natural to find reasons for postponing a difficult task—but undesirable. The more frequently the phobic confronts the situation he is afraid of, and the more time he spends in that situation, the faster his progress. It is not necessary that exposure therapy proceed at a breakneck pace, but if it proceeds too slowly, treatment does not work at all. What the patient has learned in his last encounter fades from memory, and all he can think about the next time is the many previous times he was panicky in that place and ran away.

f. On the other hand, a task that seems too difficult can be broken down into easier steps. Such a task—a "stuck point"—can appear at any point along the way of treatment. A phobic who has steadily expanded the perimeter in which he can function comfortably may come nevertheless to a situation which seems beyond him, usually because of especially awful memories of having been panicky in those circumstances in the past. Sometimes such a place, or task, can be overcome by addressing it a little bit at a time.

Even after Millie was comfortable going into small shops and stores, she still found herself afraid of a particular large department store. It was a place where she had once embarrassed herself in front of a friend— or so she thought—by being unable to try on a dress. On at least two other occasions she had had panic attacks as soon as she got in the door. Now she felt uncomfortable just sitting in her car in the parking lot. By an effort of will she could get to the store's entrance but no further. Millie got past this "stuck point" very slowly, first by standing outside the entrance with a helper, sometimes for as long as an hour, then just inside the entrance, keeping in mind that whenever she wished she could leave. Next she came into the store and purchased something on a nearby counter, still in the presence of her helper. In such a way she progressed almost imperceptibly throughout the store, first with her helper, then by herself. In the end the store had become no more frightening to her than any other place.

Other obstacles can be overcome in a similarly stepwise fashion, even such tasks that at first glance seem to defy halfway measures such as crossing a bridge or flying in an airplane.

As an example, here are steps to cross an uncrossable bridge:

i. Listening to someone who has already been across the bridge describe it—how long it is, how crowded, and so forth.

ii. Going to the bridge and looking at it. (Yes, just looking.)

iii. Walking part of the way across the bridge, then back.

iv. Driving across the bridge with a helper.

v. Meeting the helper at the other end of the bridge.

vi. Driving across the bridge by oneself.

Having managed for the first time to enter a difficult situation, the phobic should "lock in" that success by quickly going back into the situation again and again, staying for longer and longer periods of time.

3. *Don't be afraid of the panic.* Panic comes automatically in response to certain circumstances and associations and goes away promptly. It is not the panic itself but the attempt to avoid the panicky feelings by withdrawal that is the cause of the phobic condition. Retreating from a dangerous place invests other places reminiscent of that first place with danger, places where the phobic had previously felt safe. Soon there is no place that is safe. And the panic attacks come anyway. During exposure therapy the phobic must expect to get panicky from time to time.

A subtle distinction may be drawn in this connection:

The phobic cannot prevent the panic from coming, *but he can learn to make it go away.* Ordinarily, at the moment of becoming panicky, certain stereotyped thoughts come forcefully to mind:

· What if I am trapped here?
· What if these physical symptoms worsen?
· What if I lose control of my mind?
· What if I scream or embarrass myself some other way?

As a result, the frightened feeling seems to soar uncontrollably, or seems controllable only by leaving promptly. However, with practice, the phobic can learn to turn his mind from these distressing thoughts to others. First of all he should try to remember:

a. The panic is only a feeling; while it is certainly terrible, it is not dangerous to physical or emotional health, or in any other way.

b. At its worst the feeling usually lasts no more than a minute or two, although the panic may return again briefly a few minutes later and repeatedly over a period (rarely) of a few hours, only to leave again. Sometimes then the affected person has a sense of being continuously panicky. However, more careful observation shows that impression is wrong.

Psychiatrists ordinarily do not recommend to patients that they attempt to control their thoughts or feelings. Sad feelings, for example, cannot be expunged by advice to "look on the bright side." Troubling thoughts cannot be turned away by an effort of will alone. The more someone tries not to think a particular thought, the more it seems to come to mind. Trying not to imagine a purple cow brings forth an image of a purple cow, however unlikely or irrelevant a purple cow may be. What is plainly under someone's control, to some extent at least, is his behavior. Someone chronically depressed may learn to behave in such a way that his life becomes less depressing. Doing so, however, requires courage or, at least, a certain optimism. Consequently, treatment for this sort of long-term depression—usually a psychoanalytically-oriented therapy—becomes a protracted effort to alter simultaneously both morale and behavior. Something similar underlies the exposure therapy of phobias. The patient is encouraged first of all to remain in the phobic situation long enough to learn that he *can* remain there. But along the way he has to control his panicky thoughts just long enough to discover he *can* control them—or, more precisely, just for the few minutes it takes before the panic recedes. *Anything that turns the phobic's attention from the panic—from the sense of spiraling fear and impending disaster—will work.* And, to this small extent at least, experience indicates that someone can learn to control his feelings and thoughts.

Rather than turning one's attention away from the panic, it seems in some subtle way easier to turn one's attention *toward* something else. Activities that are inherently interesting work best as a distraction.

a. *Conversation:* There is almost always opportunity to interact with other people, by talking, for example. Someone panicky in a car can talk to another person riding alongside, or if no one is present, to someone within reach of a CB radio. Someone waiting on line at a bank or a supermarket can talk to someone else on line. In a department store, a salesperson is always available. Talking is better than listening. Standing in a group while others talk may not be sufficient distraction.

b. *Engaging in an activity that requires thought,* such as:

- Balancing a checkbook;
- Figuring out a puzzle;
- Attending to the circumstances that may have stimulated the panic or searching for the stray thought that may have provoked the attack;

- Writing a running account of the panic attack as the feeling of anxiety waxes and wanes;
- Adding the cost of items that the person is considering purchasing;
- Timing the panicky feelings, the length of a particular red light, or how long it takes to cross a bridge or ride from floor to floor in an elevator.

c. *Observing systematically:* Someone who becomes panicky while riding on a train can look out the window at the countryside keeping track, perhaps, of the various homes and communities or of particular shops. Sometimes he can involve himself in his imagination with the people who live and work there. Or he can listen to the sounds of the train itself, trying to fit music to the rhythm of the wheels. Someone waiting nervously during a wedding reception can distract himself by taking note of the decorations, the dress of the wedding party, the food, the smell of the flowers, or the texture of the wooden benches. It is important that such observations be *systematic*. Looking around randomly demands too little attention to distract the phobic effectively from his panic.

d. *Engaging in specific repetitive behaviors*, such as:

- Counting the people within view, the bumps on a steering wheel, or the out-of-state license plates on passing cars;
- Unwrapping chewing gum;
- Pinching oneself;
- Snapping a rubber band or playing with a paper clip.

Some people can involve themselves in these simple actions long enough for the panic to subside, but obviously any task that has so little inherent interest may not serve reliably as a distraction from the overwhelming fear and racing thoughts that are the panic attack.

But such tasks are easier to do. When a patient first confronts his panic, usually all the complicated, intellectual undertakings he has planned fly right out of mind. For this reason it is a good idea to carry around a list of things to do to distract oneself. Just running a finger down the list tends to help after a while, and so do these other mechanical tasks. Relaxation exercises or other kinds of exercise may be considered under this heading. They work no less well but probably no better than other kinds of repetitive behavior.*

4. *Be active.* At the heart of the phobic experience is the sense of being trapped or helpless. Consequently, the panicky feelings strike most often when the phobic is forced—seemingly forced—to remain passively and quietly in one place. Unfortunately, these situations are common. The phobic has to sit quietly in church, in restaurants, and under hair-dryers, and has to stand quietly in a line at a department store, on an elevator, and on a subway.

But the phobic can feel trapped simply by someone engaging him in a conversation. He seems to have few of the alternatives available to ordinary people, i.e., making an excuse and leaving. It is important, therefore, to find ways of being active rather than passive. Even during these quiet moments there are things the phobic can find to do. Some of them are mentioned above. It is the fact that they require him to become active that underlies their usefulness. They work because they allow the phobic to escape from ruminating into activity.

In these respects the phobic should cultivate a defiant attitude. If his natural inclination is to drive slowly during a panic attack, he should purposely speed up a little. If his tendency is to hurry in order to get where he is going as quickly as possible, he should purposely slow down. Some-

---

* Exercises that do work less well are those that involve breathing. The phobic is likely in the first place to worry about breathing too much or too little. Focusing his attention on this automatic, self-correcting process serves sometimes to make him still more anxious and self-conscious.

one who feels that he must turn back immediately from the phobic situation should purposely first go a little farther the other way. In the process he will come to recognize more clearly that *he is in control*—both of the vehicle, if he is driving, and of himself. Similarly, someone afraid of getting stuck in an elevator will have a better sense of its reliability by jumping up and down in it—testing it and challenging his fears at the same time.

Perhaps because the unconscious conflict underlying the panic attack may have to do with anger, expressing anger often seems to mitigate the panicky feelings. More than one prim, middle-aged lady has reported to me that she finds herself cursing under her breath when she stands in front of a bank of elevators—and feeling better as a result. A phobic is usually well on the way to recovery when he announces to me—and to himself—that he doesn't give a damn if he has a heart attack or goes crazy or whatever, he's going straight ahead into that phobic situation, no matter what! Pretending to feel that way doesn't help, though. It is a statement of the patient's determination to struggle actively against his condition; but it comes sincerely only late in treatment when he has come to understand that in fact he is not going to go crazy or suffer a heart attack.

5. *Practice.* It must be understood from the outset of treatment that there can be no improvement without practice. None of the devices suggested above work without practice. Learning takes place only a little at a time. A phobic learns not to be frightened in a particular situation only by exposing himself over and over to those circumstances. He learns not to be afraid of the panic only by becoming panicky over and over again, and discovering over and over that there is nothing to be afraid of. The phobic should not expect too much from himself initially. The suggestions offered above do not work reliably or to any great extent until they have been practiced. But what serves in the beginning to lower the level of anxiety only

to a small extent will later on have more and more of an effect, until the panic itself becomes controllable.

The phobic should practice dealing with the phobic situations—and with the possibility of becoming panicky—every day. It is not possible to spend too much time practicing. The worst that will happen if someone does "too much"—confronts one frightening situation after another—is that he may return home that evening shaken and exhausted. It is not a pleasant feeling, nor is it required for a successful treatment, but neither is it destructive to treatment. What is destructive is doing too little. Practicing one day a week is too little to allow any progress at all. Besides, facing up to a phobia so slowly is in the end more painful, like entering into a cold pool of water just a little bit at a time. On the other hand, there is no precise timetable for recovery. Some people working slowly but steadily may take a long time to get better but may recover completely nevertheless.

6. *Be realistic and fair to yourself.* Phobics tend to think too little of themselves and expect too much. Because they must avoid certain ordinary places, they regard themselves as ineffectual and ridiculous. No matter how successful they may be in all other areas of their lives, they regard themselves as failures. Similarly, they make little of every step they take along the way of getting better. Someone who is able after considerable effort to drive unaccompanied to the other end of town dismisses that achievement because he really wants to be free to drive across the country—even when, only a few weeks before, he was unable to drive at all! Driving across town, it usually turns out, is halfway to driving across the country. It is the accumulation of small successes that leads ultimately to a full recovery. Courage is required, but so is patience.

Phobics, who tend to get demoralized too easily, should take careful note of their successes. It sometimes seems that every minor failure weighs in their minds equally with a half-dozen successes. It is precisely the memory of these occasional failures, and all those that preceded treatment, that makes difficult further attempts to overcome the phobia. As the phobic progresses, therefore, he should keep track of how much more he can do now than he could do previously. He should not compare himself to someone who was never phobic in the first place. In order to keep in mind these successes, it is important to know what constitutes success:

Being able to enter into a phobic situation that was previously impossible.

Being able to go just a little farther into a phobic situation than the day before.

Being able to stay in that situation just a moment longer.

Being able by a conscious effort to lower the level of anxiety or panic, however slightly or briefly.

Being able to tolerate the panic a moment longer.

Even when the phobic recognizes his successes, he is likely to dismiss them as accidental:

"Sure, I stayed through the party, but only because I met this person who talked a lot."

"I was able to address the group, but only because it was a small group and the room was dark and the air conditioner was making a noise in the background that distracted me."

It turns out there is always some unusual and unanticipated circumstance that makes the phobic situation more tolerable. Taking advantage of these unforeseen distractions is one way the phobic learns to master his anxiety. Remembering these occasions as victories, which they truly are, encourages him to enter into that phobic situation the next time.

Recovery does not mean, of course, that the phobic will not be frightened by being in a truly frightening situation. Someone who reports with disappointment that he can still get "panicky" when the automobile he is driving skids on an icy road is confusing the emotional reaction of panic with plain fear, an appropriate and useful reaction to danger. In any case, the phobic cannot measure his progress by what he feels at any particular moment, but by what he can do. Sometimes, paradoxically, a patient making steady progress in treatment becomes depressed or especially anxious for a period of a few days. These reactions are temporary, and unless they have some other more profound cause, they disappear ultimately as the phobia recedes further.

7. *Use a helper.* Like most difficult things in life, overcoming a phobia is accomplished more easily with help from other people. Someone who is familiar with the condition—ideally, someone who has himself recovered from a phobia—is best able to manage the complicated business of cajoling and encouraging the patient to face his fears, at the same time being patient enough not to press him beyond his capacity. A good friend familiar with the principles of treatment, a spouse, or even a parent can serve effectively as a helper.

The service a helper or phobia aide can provide is two-fold:

a. He accompanies the patient into the phobic situation. By his presence alone he helps to distract the phobic from the various disasters he is prone to imagine— "What if the escalator gets stuck?" "What if we lose our way?"—and also distract him from the panic itself. The helper is someone to talk to. At those moments a phobic is likely, at least initially, to forget everything he has learned about the treatment of phobias, but the helper is there to remind him.

b. He encourages the patient. Phobics get discouraged very easily. Low morale seems to be an integral part of the condition. The helper can remind the phobic to give himself credit for what he has already achieved and point out what he can reasonably expect to do in the future. Enthusiasm is important. In particular, he can help plan reasonable goals for each day's practice session, keeping in mind that progress in therapy can be slow as long as it is steady. A person does not have to be pushed into the deep end of the pool or off a high diving board in order to learn how to swim.

The helper may make suggestions, but in determining what is possible on a particular occasion, the phobic himself must be the final judge. An inexperienced aide sometimes pressures a patient into going further than he really can on the basis of his having gone that far the previous day. But what is doable one day may not be doable the next because of some subtle change of circumstance. On the other hand, sometimes a helper, perhaps an ex-phobic, out of an excessive concern for the phobic's distress, may hesitate allowing the patient to go as fast as he feels he can. This is also undesirable. The phobic is sensitive to other people's anxieties and is easily deterred.

Two more obvious pitfalls for a helper are: sneering at the small successes that are so crucial to an eventual recovery, or, more forgivable because it is out of sympathy for the phobic's anguish, doing for him many things that he could very well do for himself, which serves in the long run to make him feel still less competent.

8. *Group support.* Someone experiencing a panic attack for the first time cannot understand exactly what is happening to him. The symptoms are so remarkable and diverse, he usually concludes that he is suffering from either a serious physical illness or mental illness. After the phobia is fully developed, by which time he has usually seen a number of different doctors who have made a variety of different diagnoses, he is likely to conclude that he has an obscure and unfathomable disease, something unique to him. Even when he comes to understand finally that his illness is agoraphobia, he still thinks that no one has ever suffered precisely as he has—the same sort of symptoms, perhaps, but not that bad—for no one who felt that awful could possibly have managed to tolerate such feelings long enough to get well! It is very helpful, therefore, for a phobic to participate in group meetings with

other phobics as part of his treatment. In that setting he will come to understand that his illness is common, perhaps more severe than some but no more severe than some others. More important, seeing other phobics improve week by week encourages him to think that treatment will help him also. And he may learn from them the strategies that they have found helpful in dealing with their phobias. If the group includes ex-phobics, so much the better. They can offer the benefit of their experience and also offer by their presence unmistakable testimony to the fact that phobias can be cured.

Unfortunately, many phobics have no such treatment group available to them. The number of these clinics is small, and they tend to be located in urban areas, whereas agoraphobia is a common and widespread condition. In addition, some phobics are housebound and unable to attend such a meeting if it were held across the street. In order to meet the needs of all those phobics who have no access to such a treatment program, a home-centered tape program was developed by the White Plains Hospital Phobia Clinic. The discussion in these unrehearsed tape recordings illustrates the principles of treatment in considerable detail. They can become the basis for a number of phobics getting together and forming their own self-help group.

9. *Admit to others that you are phobic.* It is probably impossible for anyone to change without first being able to know himself and accept himself the way he is. There is no way to address any weakness or failing without first being able to face up to it. Most phobics assert that they know only too well they are phobic; however, their ability to come truly to terms with their condition should be judged by one standard only: their readiness to admit to it and to explain it to others. This account does not have to be an elaborate statement of all their fears or their sense of inadequacy. The phobic does not have to label himself "phobic," a term which is not likely to mean anything to other people. But somehow he has to convey to them something

of his anxieties. A remark such as: "I feel uncomfortable in crowded places like this" or "I'm uneasy sitting here because I get a trapped feeling," is enough.

Someone not phobic would think such advice is simple enough to follow, but admissions of this kind are painful to most phobics and apparently impossible to some. There are those who work desperately hard to overcome their fear of the phobic situation but nevertheless balk at this seemingly much easier part of treatment. It is as if by speaking about their phobia they were revealing some awful ugliness, making themselves vulnerable to everyone's contempt. "I'll wait until I get better, and then I can tell everyone I'm an ex-phobic," they suggest. Unfortunately, experience makes plain that in fact no one is entirely cured without his first being frank with friends and family about his condition.*

Frankness serves a number of purposes. A phobic accompanied into the phobic situation by a friend will invariably feel more comfortable if he can speak openly to that person about his uneasiness. Spared the effort of having to hide his feelings, he will be able more successfully to pay attention to the real world around him. Often the friend will involve him in a discussion that serves to distract him further from his phobic preoccupations. Finally, he knows there is an escape. Because he can leave the situation temporarily without having to make up an excuse, it becomes possible, paradoxically, to stay. A student who is phobic of classrooms will almost always be able to remain through a particular class if he is willing to explain to the teacher ahead of time that he is phobic and may have to leave briefly from time to time.

Even after coming to believe that being open with others in such a way is important, some phobics still demur.

---

* Work is an exception. It is not sensible to be frank with employers about emotional or medical problems, or indeed any other problems. Doing so distracts attention from the worker's performance, which is the only proper measure of his abilities.

"These things can't be kept confidential," they point out to me, "and in the real world* there are nasty people who gossip and who will use anything—any sign of weakness or failure—against you."

Actually, the responses received by phobics to this sort of confidence are, as I have indicated before, sometimes indifferent but for the most part sympathetic. The few who do indeed respond badly will indeed "use *anything* against you." They look down on everybody for all sorts of reasons and "giving them more ammunition" does not matter one way or the other. Besides, whoever listens to them knows very well the sort of people they are and is not likely to pay much attention. In short, there is no social stigma to being phobic.

By being frank, therefore, the phobic comes to believe through his own experience that in the eyes of others being phobic is not shameful, but rather understandable as an expression of fears that everyone feels to some extent.

10. *Finish Treatment.* If the proper standard for improvement in treatment is the growing ability to tolerate phobic situations and especially the ability to tolerate the panic itself, then the proper standard for cure is the willingness and ability to outlast the panicky feelings *wherever they may occur.* By stubborn application of these principles of treatment there surely does come a time when the affected person—although still experiencing attacks of panic intermittently—is no longer afraid of the panic. At that point the phobic has finally come to understand that the attack is not of itself dangerous. It does not lead to a physical or mental impairment, and it does not drive the phobic into behaving irrationally. It cannot be said that the phobic has learned this once and for all, however, unless it can be seen to apply in all circumstances, everywhere.

But before then there comes a time in treatment when phobics are almost all better, but not quite. They work and

* As opposed to the ivory-tower world in which I live.

go about socially, and they drive usually within a wide perimeter without feeling anxious at all except for occasional short-lived and widely spaced episodes of panic. They often forget how terribly affected they once were by their illness. Nevertheless, they still hesitate to finish treatment. They reserve—almost perversely—certain areas where they will not go.

"I am doing everything I want to do," someone may say. "Why do I need to drive across that particular bridge?" . . . "fly in an airplane?" . . . "take a train trip?" . . . "give a party for my in-laws?"

"You must," I explain, "just because you're still afraid to."

It is not necessary for phobics to throw themselves into activities that are inherently dangerous or that even seem to them to be truly dangerous—such as sky-diving or walking through a bad neighborhood—but if they avoid a situation simply because they feel that in that special setting they may still get panicky, it means that on some level they are still afraid of the panic attack. Many patients suspend treatment at this point. If they are very active and practice every day within the perimeter in which they are able to live comfortably, they can continue in this way, largely untroubled, indefinitely. However, they are likely to remain always concerned that some unforeseen circumstance will unpredictably precipitate them into the special situation that is still intolerable to them. Also, they are prone to relapse. If illness or some other circumstance keeps them at home for a few weeks, they are likely to find it difficult once again to enter into all those situations to which they adjusted so painfully and with so much effort in the past. For this reason the phobic should make that last persistent effort needed to get better once and for all.

These rules of treatment are elaborated and made plain in the following chapters. Reference is not made to them by number since they are not intended as empty formulae but as guiding principles. Still, there is nothing said or done throughout treatment that does not embody them.

Medication

No chapter on the treatment of agoraphobia would be complete without some discussion of medication, if for no other reason than medication is so frequently prescribed.

Phobic patients tend to have an ambivalent attitude toward the use of medicine. On one hand, they are often afraid of using drugs, thinking the drugs will precipitate in them all kinds of frightening or uncontrollable feelings. Told to take an antihistamine or even an aspirin, they may break it in half and agonize for an hour or so before taking it. Immediately after they may feel dizzy or experience an exacerbation of any of the feelings they experience ordinarily as part of a panic attack.

On the other hand, other phobic patients—and sometimes the same phobic patients—become overly dependent on drugs, particularly the minor tranquilizers. They feel insecure unless they are carrying these drugs around with them constantly, often with a bottle of water so they can take a pill the instant they need one. Usually they feel better as soon as they swallow the pill, *even though they know the medication takes a half hour or longer to be absorbed.*

Both of these contrasting behaviors are founded on the idea—an *incorrect* idea—that medication, all medications, are extremely potent. The fact is that most of them are not addicting or dangerous in the doses usually prescribed. Whether they are very useful or not is another question. Certainly there are some patients who are helped by drugs, but it is debatable whether these agents are of primary importance in treatment or indicated simply as an adjunct to exposure therapy. A growing literature has been published on both sides.* What follows is a personal view of the role medication plays in the management of agoraphobia.

There are three situations in which one would hope medication would prove useful:

1. To lessen the general level of anxiety that commonly troubles the phobic during each day, even when he is not steeling himself to confront the phobic situation. Most psychoactive drugs have been tried for this purpose. The major tranquilizers have not proven helpful. Usually the phobic feels drugged and, consequently, still more uncomfortable. Some people feel, paradoxically, more anxious the more sedated they are. Besides, the side effects of these drugs are more unsettling to phobics than to most people for the reasons given previously. The most commonly prescribed medications used to combat anxiety are the minor tranquilizers, particularly the benzodiazepines, one of which is Valium. The advantages of such drugs are that they have relatively few side effects, are reasonably safe and, to some extent, they work. At least they produce an effect that anxious people report as calming—and some others report as a "high."† The effect is short-lived and does not seem to encourage most phobics to systematically approach those situations that frighten them. The disadvantages of these drugs, in my opinion, far outweigh the momentary benefit:

   a. Although true addiction is uncommon, the drugs encourage a psychological dependence that continues long past the few weeks for which their use is intended. Some people feel they cannot get up in the morning without first taking a Valium.

* For contrasting views on this subject see the debate in pages 341–343, "Letters to the Editor," of the *New England Journal of Medicine*, Vol. 308, Feb. 10, 1983. Also see the representative bibliography on page 229.

† These are "street drugs." One recent year over half the patients on Methadone maintenance in Westchester County, New York, were also taking Valium in order to get "high." Whether the effect of the drug is calming or exhilarating may depend to some extent on the expectation of the patient.

b. In some people the prolonged use of minor tranquilizers can cause or worsen depression, a condition that often complicates the phobic disorders. Someone whose life is as constrained as that of the typical phobic doesn't need an additional reason to feel bad.

c. Most important of all, the phobic who manages by a special effort to confront a frightening situation, but who is taking these drugs, usually convinces himself that it is only because of these drugs that he is successful. He imagines he is less capable than he really is, and learns nothing from his successes. Actually, the pharmacological effect of such drugs is minor.* It is the patient's expectation that the drug will somehow work that lends it importance. The persistent use of these drugs works against treatment since they encourage the phobic to feel weak and inept.

2. To prevent or relieve the panic attack itself. The two major classes of antidepressant drugs are used for this purpose. They have been reported by certain investigators to block the panic attack, making the task of approaching the phobic situation much easier. If they really did work reliably in such a way, there would still be reason to write this book. Even those clinicians who regard these drugs as the keystone to treatment recognize that the phobia does not necessarily go away when the panic attacks are blocked. Desensitization to the phobic situation may still be required. Still, it is true that the phobia is sustained primarily by the fear of becoming panicky. It would be easier to ward off the feeling with a pill than undertake the painful process described in these chapters. In my experience, though, most patients on these medications continue to re-

---

* A relatively new drug of this class, alprazolam (Xanax), has been reported to be more effective by itself or in combination with other drugs. Most studies seem to suggest, however, that symptoms return whenever the medication is withdrawn. In any case, as with every other new drug, it is not possible to know for certain whether the good results reported initially will hold up with longer experience. See Chapter 8.

port panic attacks nevertheless, certainly from time to time and usually just as intense as ever. And perhaps as many as 20 percent of phobic patients refuse to take them in any case because they find their side effects intolerable. Another considerable number relapse as soon as the medication is withdrawn! It may be, however, that there is a subgroup of phobic patients—perhaps some less severely ill than those who come to the Phobic Clinic—who do indeed show a consistent response to the antidepressants. So it is reasonable to give them a try. Used with proper supervision they are safe and do not encourage a psychological dependence, as do the minor tranquilizers.

There is one specific clinical situation where antidepressant medications are very helpful, if not crucial. Most phobics wake up anxious and uneasy on days when they have to confront a difficult task, but feel relatively well on other mornings. However, should a phobic wake up *every* morning in the midst of a panic that lasts off and on for hours, only to improve possibly in the evening, and should he also over the course of weeks lose his appetite to the point of losing weight, he would then probably be suffering from a superimposed depression—even if he doesn't report that he is subjectively depressed! Under those circumstances he is very likely to respond dramatically to these drugs, experiencing, after a number of days or a few weeks, an elevation of mood, a marked lessening in agitation and restlessness, and a decrease in the number of panic attacks.*

3. To help the phobic person confront a particularly difficult task. Exposure therapy demands that the phobic subject himself time and again to painful experiences. The most difficult are usually those occasions when he approaches a phobic situation for the first time—a wedding, a train ride, an airplane flight—and anything that serves to make that task easier is allowable. Sooner or later the phobic must learn that he can go anywhere and do anything

* For a more detailed discussion of this issue, see Chapter 8.

that other people can, *whether or not he is panicky;* and he must know that he can do it on his own, without drugs. But he doesn't have to come to that understanding all at once. If the prospect of a first plane trip is made less threatening by taking a pill first or a couple of martinis in the travelers' lounge, that's fine. For this purpose any accustomed tranquilizer will serve.

In summary, medication may have a role in the treatment of agoraphobia, but it cannot by itself teach people to lead less frightened lives. Only repeated exposure to the phobic situation and to the panic itself will give the affected person confidence that no matter what happens to him in the future—should he get panicky again one day—he will nevertheless never again become phobic. He will never again have to run away.

Chapter 3

EIGHT STAGES OF RECOVERY

It is easy to memorize a set of treatment principles, even to understand them, but learning how to make use of them is difficult. Knowing in principle how plumbing works is not the same thing as knowing how to put together a system of pipes. The following sections are an attempt to make explicit a practical, systematic, week-by-week program by which someone can recover from a severe phobia. Since it is modeled on the eight-week treatment program offered by the White Plains Hospital Phobia Clinic, I have divided the process of recovery, for heuristic purposes, into eight stages. Actually, a particular patient may be working his way through two or three stages at a time, usually but not necessarily in the order in which I describe them. What can be said for certain, however, is that a permanent cure means somehow traveling this route from beginning to end.

I take the liberty in this section of addressing the phobic directly.

STAGE ONE: RECOGNIZING THE FACT OF BEING PHOBIC

Obviously, proper treatment begins with the proper diagnosis. If you have read this far, you probably consider yourself phobic, but you may not be sure. For reasons described earlier, you may still be concerned that some obscure physical or mental illness is causing your symptoms. Such doubts are understandable. Sensible people come to me worried that they may have asthma, epilepsy, hyperthyroidism, heart disease—especially heart disease —or any of the other varied afflictions to which man is vulnerable. If by some chance they have a concurrent physical illness, they may attribute the symptoms of the phobia to that condition. Repeated reassurances by doctors fail to reassure. Everyone has heard of the man who leaves his doctor's office with a clean bill of health only to drop dead in the street. Doctors are not infallible.

"Maybe I didn't explain my symptoms to him in enough detail," anxious patients say to themselves.

"Maybe he didn't take the right test," they may think.

Somebody they know, it turns out, had a pheochromocytoma *for years*, and they told her it was psychological! Besides, there is this magazine article in *Good Health, Inc.* that says lots of people get low blood sugar, which can cause anxiety, weakness, depression, shaking, and sometimes loss of control—even violence. "Maybe to be on the safe side," they think, "I should eat carrots or potatoes."* These are natural concerns. It is not surprising that in the face of the pronounced physiological reaction of the panic attack, you may think such thoughts, especially if you start

---

* It is bad enough that a serious and uncommon condition such as hypoglycemia is frequently diagnosed (nineteen out of twenty times in error), but the usual diet recommended is the wrong one. Potatoes, for example, have an effect on the blood sugar similar to raw sugar.

off, as most phobics do, overly concerned about matters of health.

On the other hand, you may be one of those people who are fearful and avoid certain situations but are not sure if they are suffering from a true phobia.

"Just because I don't want to drive in city traffic or on highways, does that mean I'm phobic?"

"If I hate traveling because I always get lost, does that mean I'm phobic?"

"Just because I feel uncomfortable in church or nervous at weddings, does that mean I'm phobic?"

Yes—*if because of those feelings you avoid those places.*

"But all the people I know feel nervous at weddings, frightened driving on highways, uncomfortable in the city, and so on. Are they *all* phobic?"

Only if they are so nervous or frightened that they too avoid those places. Most of them surely will not prove to be fearful to such an extent, but some may, for phobias are very common. Of course, there may be a dangerous highway somewhere or a city—Calcutta, perhaps—where a sensible person would hesitate to go. Someone afraid of a truly dangerous situation is not phobic. Even if someone is under the mistaken impression that a particular place or thing is dangerous—a garter snake, for example—and avoids it for that reason, he is not phobic. But if someone knows very well that he is only frightened of himself, his own reaction to these things, his own uneasiness, then he does indeed have a phobia. Even in such a mild, circumscribed form, the condition should be treated because otherwise it tends to spread.

The task of this stage of treatment, then, is to determine once and for all if you are phobic.

INSTRUCTIONS

1. Read this book carefully. There are other very good descriptions of the condition in the suggested readings. Phobics tend to resemble one another to a considerable degree, and if you are phobic, you should recognize yourself in these pages. Inform yourself about the variety of phobic symptoms. However, do not expect to learn anything about yourself from reading accounts in the popular press of obscure mental or emotional illnesses. These articles are written to be intriguing, not informative, and they are not accurate. Refrain from "matching up" your symptoms with those of other people you know who have had a heart attack or some other terrible illness. Every symptom of a heart attack is the symptom of a half-dozen other illnesses as well.

2. If you are concerned that you may be suffering from a physical ailment, by all means see a doctor, someone whose judgment you trust. One doctor—maybe two—should suffice. It is very unlikely that a competent physician will miss the diagnosis of a serious physical illness. You don't have to read the medical literature yourself or recommend particular tests. He is trained for this job. If you know you are phobic or hypochondriacal but nevertheless develop a new physical symptom, consult with him again. Even people who worry too much about their health get truly ill from time to time. Besides, being reassured that there is nothing the matter with you physically is worth the time and money involved—even if the secure feeling does not last very long. Keep in mind, though, that continual visits to doctors should not be used to hide from your underlying phobia. Once you are convinced your problems are emotional, it is reasonable to visit a psychiatrist or a psychologist. There are, after all, other psychiatric conditions with

which this condition can be confused. If he confirms that you are phobic, an exposure therapy should help.

3. Try not to look for physical causes of your distress. If someone gets a panic attack one hour after drinking orange juice, it is not necessarily due to the orange juice. Similarly, a panic attack that takes place after waking from a nap is not necessarily attributable to the nap. This tendency to add two and two and come up with five is an example of the superstitious thinking that underlies most phobic ideas. The phobia itself results when a particular feeling (panic) has become associated with a particular activity or set of circumstances, just because it happened to take place once in that setting. It is as if the phobic believed the setting caused the panic, although the place may be as mundane and familiar as a movie theater or as innocuous as riding in a bus. Similarly, panic attacks may be associated with physical exercise, stomach upset, or the use of various drugs. It need not follow, however, that one is truly the cause of the other.

4. Nevertheless, take detailed notes of the circumstances in which you become anxious or panicky: what thoughts or circumstances provoke an attack, and conversely what thoughts or change of circumstances cause a lessening of anxiety. * Although the connections may exist only in your mind, as indicated above, they are important. Knowing you are phobic means knowing precisely how the phobia affects you. Important to this stage of treatment—and at many points later on—is the habit of accurate self-observation. If you are typical, you may have been phobic for years without knowing any of these things in exact detail.

---

* There are a number of times throughout this book when I recommend to the phobic that he produce a written account of one thing or another. Experience has shown that these lists or charts are important. They are a concrete reminder to the phobic person of where he has been and where he is going—and how to get there. His willingness to invest time and effort in drawing up these accounts is a good indicator of what his future progress is likely to be.

When Millie entered into treatment she made a careful inventory of her fears. The situations in which she felt uncomfortable were many. Church, or any quiet place that reminded her of church, such as a library, was intolerable. Most restaurants made her anxious but were bearable if she sat with her husband in plain sight of an exit. She could remain home alone but not overnight and not unless she was fully dressed, prepared on a moment's notice to leave for a hospital if that became necessary. The presence of any other person, even a six-year-old niece, made her feel more secure for reasons she could not explain. Although driving a car was impossible, going along as a passenger was manageable depending on who drove, who else accompanied them, how long a trip it was, the weather, and the time of day. Similarly, certain thoughts, Millie noted, were likely to provoke a panic attack: hearing of someone's sudden death, particularly from a heart attack, the thought that her husband's car might break down while he was on the road, or the fear that she herself might become lost in a strange neighborhood or somehow become incapacitated physically. The detailed description Millie drew up of her phobia filled four typewritten pages.

The variety of situations around which people can become phobic are innumerable, but the thoughts that trouble them are few:

a. The fear of dying, which is not the most basic fear but which derives usually from two other fears—the fear of being helpless, as someone immobilized in a coffin is helpless, and the fear of being alone, away forever from those people to whom one feels close.

b. The fear of being lost (literally lost, as if by making a wrong turn on a highway one can never return home).

c. The fear of losing control; for example, cursing out loud in a classroom, tearing off one's clothes in public, or falling to the ground. Some phobics are afraid of becoming violent.

d. The fear of being ridiculous or of embarrassing oneself. Revealing the phobia itself becomes an embarrassment.

Therefore, the detailed analysis you make of your phobia serves these purposes:

a. You can recognize the phobia and its effect on all aspects of your life. The disturbing picture that may emerge is a goad to action, a reason to enter vigorously into treatment.

b. You can see each particular fear in terms of the larger context of the phobia. Certain symptoms wax and wane more than others. These are worth noting for they are more readily attacked in the beginning of treatment.

c. The underlying meanings of certain fears become clear—the fear of being lost, being helpless, being alone, being out of control. Sometimes these concerns can be addressed directly. For example, someone who learns to assert himself effectively becomes less troubled by the sudden sense of being helpless. These fears grow out of basic problems of living.

d. When no longer diffuse and unfathomable, the phobia takes on specific outlines and becomes for that reason less frightening. Imagined illnesses and dangers tend to be scarier than real ones.

e. Finally, and most important, merely examining your illness is taking charge of it in a way. Instead of feeling buffeted by strange and unpredictable impulses, you are taking an active stance—*doing something* instead of waiting for something to happen to you. It is this precise change in psychological set that enables you finally to get well.

5. Out of those detailed notes you have taken, construct a hierarchy of fears or frightening situations. List at the bottom those you can master with a minimal effort, further up those requiring a greater effort, and at the top those situations so frightening you cannot enter into them no matter how hard you try.

The list Millie drew up at the beginning of treatment looked in part like this:

- Church, libraries, remaining at home alone overnight, eating alone in a restaurant
- Movie theaters
- Beauty parlors
- Department stores
- Restaurants—sitting at the back
- Restaurants—sitting in front
- Driving across town to visit mother-in-law
- Visiting a friend

As she progressed in treatment, she drew up other such lists, including this one:

- Church alone, sitting up front in the middle of a row
- Church alone, sitting up front in an aisle seat
- Church, sitting next to husband
- Church, sitting alone toward the back—for only a half hour
- Church alone, standing at the back throughout the whole service

For every phobic, no matter how seriously impaired he may be, there are certain activities that are comfortable and accustomed. Someone so phobic he cannot leave his bedroom still feels comfortable most of the time in that room. Millie, when she was at her worst, felt entirely at ease in her kitchen talking to her mother. * On the other hand, there is some place or set of circumstances into which by definition every phobic, no matter how mildly affected, is unable to go except with great effort. Perry, who could drive a few blocks without difficulty, could only drive accompanied by his wife and could not, no matter how hard he tried, no matter who was with him, drive across the bridge at the other end of town. In between such extremes there is a range of activities or circumstances—different from one person to the next—in which it is possible to

---

* Of course, at intervals—at least at distant intervals—a phobic will have panic attacks anywhere.

function but with a varying degree of difficulty. Some things are easy, some relatively hard. If it is your habit to manage with the least degree of discomfort—to function as much as possible at the bottom of this range—the whole range begins to slip.

Perry's driving phobia, for example, was not always so severe. There was a time when he could drive by himself for many miles, although even at the beginning he was never unaccompanied on highways. Because he found it more comfortable, however, to have his wife sit next to him, he got into the habit of having her do so. Soon he was unable to go any distance without her. Even with her along, it was easier to make social engagements nearby rather than farther away. After making such arrangements for a number of months, he found he could not go that extra distance even if he wanted to. He felt uncomfortable even under these more restricted circumstances and so had his friends visit him whenever they got together. Soon it was no longer possible for him to drive even relatively short distances. It was only because his work required him to drive every day at least one mile that his phobia stabilized at that point.

If, like Perry, you struggle with your phobia as little as possible, you will find, as he did, that what was once relatively easy to do will become difficult and what was difficult will become impossible. More important, areas in which you never had trouble functioning will be invaded by the phobia. Certain tasks that you never had trouble doing will now become difficult. New situations will become frightening. Conversely, if every day you purposely do those things hardest for you, in time they become easier, and those things that were easy at first become effortless. In short, you should always do as much as you can. During this first stage of treatment, though, concentrate on observing yourself accurately. Determine exactly the boundaries of your phobia.

FEELINGS TO COPE WITH AT THIS STAGE: doubt and distrust.

STAGE TWO: BEING WILLING TO TRY

If you are typical of most phobics, you have been trying to overcome your illness for years without success. By now you may be pessimistic that any treatment will prove helpful. Exposure therapy may seem at first glance to be no different from the rest. Unfortunately, your attitude toward therapy will affect its outcome. If you are convinced that nothing works, nothing can work. The task of this stage of treatment, therefore, is to find reason to believe and reason to try. In this regard, consider the experience of those who attended the White Plains Phobia Clinic.

The results of therapy reported by patients at the end of the Eight-Week Clinic are especially encouraging but may be unrealistic since the patients are then caught up with one another's success. The statistics reported below are a better gauge of lasting progress. They represent the results of questionnaires sent to patients six months after the conclusion of the clinic.

Follow-up on First 50 Phobia Clinics	
Total Number of Participants:	443
Total Number of Replies:	394
381 were helped	(96.7%)
13 not helped	(3.3%)
Of those who were helped:	
23 helped completely	(6%)
228 very much	(60%)
89 moderately	(23%)
41 slightly	(11%)
302 made additional progress	(77%)
314 continue to practice	(80%)

The statistics reported below are the results of queries four years after the conclusion of the clinic.

Follow-up on First 22 Phobia Clinics

Total Number of Participants:	192
Total Number of Replies:	153
144 were helped	(94%)
9 not helped	(6%)
Of those who were helped:	
11 helped completely	(8%)
73 very much	(51%)
45 moderately	(31%)
15 slightly	(10%)
115 made additional progress since 6-month follow-up	(75%)
100 continue to practice	(65%)
41 felt they had lost some of the gains made in the clinic	(27%)

In treatment that extends beyond eight weeks, such as may be conducted in a private practice, those completely cured represent a majority, and most of the remainder are moderately to markedly improved. The advantage of such an open-ended therapy is that there is time to achieve long-range goals. The disadvantage is that without the pressure of a definite time limit, the final stages of treatment tend to drag on indefinitely.

INSTRUCTIONS

1. Keep these statistics in mind. Do not imagine that the patients treated in the phobia clinic were *less* severely ill than you. The likelihood is that they were more troubled.

Most had failed at conventional psychotherapy and were unimproved by medication. They sometimes came from hundreds of miles away as a last resort. Proper treatment did not guarantee their cure, nor will it guarantee yours; but considerable improvement is likely, and complete cure is certainly possible—even when the condition is long-standing. Few illnesses respond so directly in proportion to the effort the patient makes.

2. Learn how the principles of exposure therapy work and how they are different from the previous treatments that were unsuccessful in helping you.

When phobias are of recent onset, patients usually respond to any sort of treatment or, indeed, to a simple explanation of their condition. If with medication or with supportive psychotherapy they can be persuaded not to be afraid of their panicky feelings, or at least not to run away if they do get panicky, the phobia diminishes and in time the panic attacks disappear. These may be regarded as transference cures. The patient gets well because he believes in the therapist or physician long enough to do what he needs to do in order to get well *whatever particular reason the therapist gives for that improvement.* If someone believes, for example, that breathing deeply for two minutes will make the panic go away, he may be proven right if for no other reason than panic usually goes away within that time. However, when the phobia is more advanced—a process that takes place quickly—such a cure becomes difficult. A patient may even then respond to hypnosis, or relaxation exercises, or psychoanalytic interpretation, or drugs, or any of the other myriad therapies in vogue *if at this later point the patient can be persuaded to remain in the phobic situation.* The problem is that usually he cannot be so persuaded. If therapy is founded on blind faith, it must work right away or it will not work at all. Exposure therapy, on the other hand, works by an understanding of the phobic process. Phobias develop out of certain ideas and out of a particular pattern of behavior—

avoidance. Proper treatment is directed at correcting those ideas and reversing that pattern of behavior. It is usually slow work, equivalent to crossing a stream by building a causeway one shovelful of dirt at a time. It requires more of an effort than trying to jump across. It is also more time-consuming but more certain in the end.

3. Contact ex-phobics through the Phobia Society and its various newsletters.*

During the course of a successful therapy the typical phobic patient assumes different attitudes toward his illness depending on the stage of his recovery. In the beginning he is usually very frightened, afraid among other things that he has a strange, uncommon, and unfathomable condition. At such a time it is reassuring to discover that other people are troubled the same way with the same symptoms—and they get better. Later on, as the phobic improves—and invariably gets stuck along the way from time to time—the encouragement of others who have traversed the same route is helpful. His mood might then be described as cautious optimism. Still further along, when he is greatly improved, he is likely to take on the enthusiastic manner of a religious convert, preaching optimism to those still struggling painfully with their phobias. He proselytizes among his family, friends, and neighbors, searching out those still hiding from their phobias, and in general spreading the good word. At this stage he is representative of all those sympathetic people who form self-help groups and promulgate phobia newsletters. You should contact them. Many of them make themselves available by telephone or through write-in groups. But if few among them seem to you to be completely recovered, do not get discouraged. They are as a group very much improved, but those who are entirely cured tend to go through one last transition. In that final stage they do not usually belong to the Phobia Society or write to newslet-

* See Appendix.

ters. They take little interest in other people's phobias for they have forgotten their own. They are troubled now only by all the usual worries and difficulties that invade people's lives, and these are sufficient.

4. Keep track of your successes. The motivated patient will quickly improve, but keep in mind what constitutes improvement:

    a. The growing ability to enter into a phobic situation —a few feet farther than yesterday or a minute or two longer.

    b. The ability to tolerate the panicky feelings a few moments longer before leaving.

These seemingly slight successes compound quickly so that within a week or two you will find yourself going places you have not been able to visit for years. It should not matter to you that the place is no farther than a block away. These early steps are crucial. Less effort will be required later on to conquer much greater distances. Do not judge your progress by how you feel on a particular day. You may be very anxious, panic *more* frequently than previously, and still be improving. On the other hand, you may feel entirely at ease but be no better if you have purchased that calm at the price of staying home. What matters is what you can do, not how comfortable you feel. Only after considerable improvement will you feel consistently less anxious.

In short, the goal of this stage of treatment is limited. You do not have to start off therapy with blind confidence in the measures I recommend or with an inner certainty of success, but you have to be willing to try. If you follow instructions, success follows, and confidence follows only after that.

FEELINGS TO COPE WITH AT THIS STAGE: pessimism and cynicism.

STAGE THREE: BEING OPEN AND WORKING WITH OTHERS

Almost without exception phobics are people who are easily embarrassed or made uncomfortable by the thought that others have a poor opinion of them. As a matter of general principle, they do not let on to anyone anything about their personal circumstances or feelings. It is as if they would then become vulnerable somehow. Such a point of view, often shared by other members of that person's family, would be vexing for anyone (it is not conducive to a relaxed, spontaneous life) but is quite incompatible with the requirements of exposure therapy.

Fundamental to the development of a severe phobia is the fear of an imminent loss of control during the panic attack, leading to embarrassing, perhaps even shameful behavior. To a considerable extent it is this wish to avoid an outburst—to hide his illness from everyone—that prevents the phobic from entering into certain situations where other people may be present. And the more he avoids phobic situations, the more phobic he becomes. If he takes this attitude toward everyone, no one will be able to help him. More important still, by hiding from others he can never come to accept himself—a prerequisite to change. Indeed, acceptance *means* a willingness to present oneself undisguised, warts and all, to anyone, acknowledging any weakness or deficiency. Some phobics never get past this stage. They may hide their condition from friends, even from parents. "I'll practice and get better, then I'll tell them I'm an ex-phobic," they may say. But no one can get better in such a way, no matter how hard he works. The goal of this stage of treatment, therefore, is for the phobic to explain readily to friends and to strangers also what circumstances make him uncomfortable or afraid.

INSTRUCTIONS

1. Tell your family and friends about being phobic. What is necessary is not a confession, "I am phobic," but something like, "I always feel uncomfortable traveling in airplanes," or "I feel very nervous in elevators, as if I'm trapped." If you tell someone whom you have just met that you are agoraphobic, he is not likely to know what you mean, but the feeling of being nervous or being trapped will not be strange to him. In some respects it is more helpful to speak to people you do not know than to those close to you. Their reaction may seem more sincere. Once they indicate, as most of them will, that they regard your problem as unremarkable, you are more likely to believe that that is the truth.

Although Janet had been seriously phobic for a great many years, she had let only a very few people know of her condition. One friend in particular had always seemed to her intolerant of weakness, even ordinary weaknesses such as drinking two cocktails before dinner, so that Janet was convinced the woman would find her inability to remain alone at home overnight especially ridiculous. There came a time in treatment, however, when Janet realized that in order to get well she would have to face the truth by speaking of it to others, to everyone in her life, even those who might be unsympathetic. When the occasion finally arrived, it was unpremeditated. The two women were shopping together in a clothing store, an activity that would have been impossible for Janet two months before when she first started treatment.

"John is going away tonight," Janet said, speaking of a business trip her husband was committed to making and which she had been dreading for weeks.

"Yes?" said her friend, looking at a dress.

"I always feel uncomfortable when I'm all alone at night," Janet went on nervously. "I hear every little sound and noise.

After a while I begin to feel anxious and panicky like something awful is going to happen."

"When I feel like that," her friend remarked absentmindedly, holding the dress up against her to see if it fit, "I always call up someone. That way it seems as though I'm safe."

All that worry for nothing. Almost always phobic fears are readily understandable to others.

People you are close to should know more about your phobia than that you are uneasy in certain situations. Begin by telling them what circumstances upset you and to what extent. Explain in detail how the phobia affects your life, specifically where you can go, where you cannot go, and where you can go only with difficulty. You do not have to offer a running account of how anxious you feel minute by minute, but if you are especially anxious at times when you are in their company, you should tell them. If there is a social occasion that you would like to attend with them, but feel you may not be able to remain very long, explain the situation. They should understand about phobias in general and about your phobia in particular. They should know what to expect. They should not be surprised if you have to leave suddenly. The important advantages of being frank, which were described earlier, may strike you at first as dubious and theoretical, but the fact is that no one gets better without being open. The more exceptions you make to this rule, the more uncertain your recovery.

"My mother-in-law? You want me to tell *her?* You don't know the way she is. She'll just look at me as if I'm crazy, and explaining won't do any good. I already have enough troubles with her. Besides, I don't even like the woman. I don't have anything to do with her."

Well, then, why not tell her?

"I don't need any unnecessary aggravation."

But it is necessary, one more painful facet of what is at best an uncomfortable and difficult treatment.

In many cases, speaking frankly is only admitting openly what everyone already knows.

2. Get a helper. It may be easier at first to acknowledge your phobia to someone who is familiar with the condition. Few people will look down on you for suffering from what seems to them only an exaggeration of fears they themselves have known, but certainly no knowledgeable person will. Someone who knows about phobias and about their treatment can also be very helpful in other ways. Ideally, the helper or phobia aide should be an ex-phobic. A growing number of trained people are serving in this capacity. Their names can usually be obtained from your local branch of the Phobia Society of America. Should no such person be available to you, choose a sympathetic friend who is willing to learn how to be an aide and who has the time to work with you at least two or three hours a week—the more time the better. Explain your symptoms to him. The specific role of the helper is described on pages 162–176. Keep in mind that a phobia aide can help to define the tasks of treatment stage by stage, but ultimately you are the one who has to do the work. He can describe to you his own, more objective view of the illness, but you have to be willing to listen.

3. If possible, join together in a group with other phobics. There are perhaps ten million phobics in the United States alone, and many groups have already sprung up. Some have been started by phobia aides but many others by ordinary people who happen to live in the same neighborhoods.

At the same time Perry entered therapy he began meeting with other phobic patients who had formed a self-help group a few months previously. Among them was an artist who had a fear of bridges, a man who owned a construction company but was afraid of heights, an agoraphobic housewife who had raised six children (all of whom had professional degrees), and a well-known newscaster, also agoraphobic. Perry, who had always thought of his phobia as shameful and ridiculous, noticed at once that at least in this protected setting each person spoke openly about his or her symptoms, without embarrassment, even though they were all at least as phobic as he was. He saw too that they were all successful and capable outside the sphere of their phobias, instead of the weaklings and failures he imagined all phobics to be, especially himself. It was only after his first meeting with them that he managed the courage to tell his wife the full extent of his fears. As he saw the others improve from week to week, he began to believe for the first time that he too could get well. Indeed, it was by following closely in their footsteps, avoiding their mistakes, doing what had worked for them, that he was able to get well.

4. Participate *actively* in the phobia society. Send for the various newsletters.* The letters written by other phobics to these journals are for the most part reassuring and give evidence that improvement comes with proper treatment. The ideas expressed are helpful and represent collectively the concerns, strategies, and wisdom of a large self-help group. They have something to teach you. And you should write in yourself; you have something useful to say. Your experience, even at the beginnings of treatment, will prove helpful to others. Remember, implicit in the mere act of writing about yourself is the active stance you must take in treatment. Saying something about yourself is the beginning of taking charge of yourself. There are also self-help telephone networks in different areas of the country, and you are invited to call these numbers.

5. Finally, use the special people in your life as special helpers. There is for everyone a privileged person, someone trusted and influential beyond all others. For most phobics—indeed, for most people in general—that person is a parent or a spouse, occasionally a grown child. According to the usual psychodynamic mythology, the phobic is *too* dependent on this person and in fact is a phobic precisely as a way of maintaining that dependent relationship. This is nonsense. There are some who fall into unhealthy and destructive relationships of this sort but almost always as the *result* of the phobia, and most phobics do not resem-

* See Appendix.

ble this caricature. If you avoid working with a parent or a spouse because of this prejudice, because you are anxious not to seem too dependent or clinging, you will be giving up a valuable resource.*

There are potential problems, though, in working with someone to whom you are closely tied emotionally. On one hand, that person may try to do too much for you, hesitating more than he should to bring you into difficult and painful situations. On the other hand, he may be rooting too hard for you to get well and therefore expect too much too soon. And there is always a troublesome tendency for other aspects of such a close relationship to intrude into the helping process. A previous quarrel about an overcooked dinner, for instance, may make practicing together difficult. Conversely, the tedious and occasionally nerve-wracking effort that practice sessions entail may have its own undesirable effect on family relationships. In some families these relationships are so precarious that this extra burden should not be taken up. Still, who else can you count on reliably day after day and week after week?

Do not feel guilty imposing on your spouse or mother for the time required to practice effectively, ideally an hour or two every day. Keep in mind that their best interests lie in your getting well as fast as possible. If you remain phobic, they will waste much more time in the long run doing things for you that you would otherwise be able to do for yourself. And, of course, they have that paramount motive —the wish that you become free of a terrible and quite unnecessary anguish.

FEELINGS TO COPE WITH AT THIS STAGE: shame, embarrassment, and false pride.

---

* The role of the family and the helper in particular is examined in detail in a later chapter.

Chapter 4

STAGE FOUR: PRACTICING—JUST A FEW FEET FARTHER, JUST A LITTLE WHILE LONGER

Reading this book or any other book is not by itself going to cure anyone. Neither will listening to a therapist in the safe haven of his office. What needs to be learned to get over a phobia—that the phobic situation is not truly dangerous and that the panic attack itself is not dangerous —can be learned once and for all only in the phobic situation, a little at a time, in measured steps. Unfortunately, the naive experience of the phobic situation is also not enough. If it were, no one would be phobic for long. Overcome again and again by a sudden sense of impending doom, the phobic comes to recognize soon enough that that irrational fear, that panic, is never followed by a disaster, physical, emotional or any other kind. Why, then, does he still get just as anxious the next time? If he has been repeatedly in a phobic situation before, and knows very well there is nothing to be afraid of, why does he still avoid that place or that thing? It seems that the sensation is so overwhelming, at least to someone already inclined to be fearful by his upbringing, that reality is forgotten. More to the point, the "reality" the phobic experiences is of extraordinary discomfort, repeated frequently if not unfailingly, and it is that unequivocal distress that allows the phobia to persist. In this sense, the explanation the phobic gives to himself and to others of his fears is not relevant or at the focus of treatment. The phobia is not responsive in any case to reasoned argument or unstructured experience, however frequently repeated. But it is possible to examine the world and the phobic situation anew. Approached properly, step by step, the phobic reaction becomes recognizable as coming from within, not pertaining really to any particular place, or thing, or set of circumstances. The sense of unpleasant anticipation, the familiar anxiety when entering seemingly impossible situations and, finally, the panic itself all become controllable. Specifically, the phobic experiences the phobic situation in such a slow, measured way that there is little opportunity to get terrified. Not having been frightened yesterday or the day before, perhaps the entire week before, he no longer expects to be frightened. Consequently, there comes a time eventually when he is no longer frightened in that situation. Not ever. Similarly, the feeling of panic itself loses its ability to terrify. This final, crucial change comes when the phobic learns—once again a little at a time and from his own experience—that the panic attack is limited and controllable. It is limited both in the sense of not worsening past a certain point and in not persisting at that extreme point for more than a minute or two before subsiding. It is controllable in the ordinary sense: The affected person learns how to diminish the feeling and in the end to banish it altogether. But the techniques required work only after long practice and depend on the growing awareness that there is nothing to be afraid of. In order for the process to work at all, though, it must proceed at a certain pace.

Pacing

Before starting to practice, it is helpful to come to an understanding of the important issue of proper pacing, that is, the amount of time that must be invested every day and the rate at which improvement must proceed in order for recovery to take place. These comments apply not only to exposure therapy but to any other business in life that is painful and tedious in nature, unpleasant in and of itself and unrewarding except at the point when the task is finished—but worthwhile nevertheless. One example of such a chore is studying for an examination. Another is dieting. These are time-dependent tasks. In order for any such undertaking to be managed successfully, it cannot proceed at a rate so slow that the person becomes demoralized and gives up halfway through. Not finishing is tantamount to failing. Overcoming a phobia means getting over it entirely. Partial improvement is only temporary, leading eventually to a relapse or, at most, to a chronic, nagging uneasiness in which every day's activities must be weighed ahead of time to see if they are manageable.

Whether or not someone gives up prematurely depends on three factors:

1. The painfulness of the task. Some things are too awful or too painful to do even for brief periods of time—although, of course, what one person finds intolerable will not seem so to another. Exposing oneself to a phobic situation or to the panicky feelings themselves is in principle never too difficult because it can be accomplished a little at a time, if necessary in exceedingly small steps and for very brief periods of time until some progress is obtained. But at best it is a difficult process.

2. The person's patience. No one can put up with an inherently unpleasant task forever, but some people can persist longer than others. Some phobic patients can make tiny, incremental improvements month after month and year

after year until they are cured, but most people cannot wait that long. The benefits of getting well, after all, come largely only at the end of treatment. The longer someone can persevere, therefore, the more likely he is to get well.

3. The speed with which progress is made. The more unpleasant a task and the less patient the person undertaking that task, the faster he must progress in order to have hopes of finishing. If he goes too slowly, he will fail in the end. Conversely, the faster he improves, the less chance he will become discouraged.

In short, it is very important to progress as quickly as possible. The necessary rate of recovery varies from person to person, as indicated above, but considerable improvement should take place in the first eight weeks—enough to see the light at the end of the tunnel grow bright.

INSTRUCTIONS

1. Beginning today and every day throughout treatment, enter into the phobic situation. There is no other way. No shortcut, no trick of understanding or point of view will make the experience comfortable, but neither will it be too difficult or too painful. Begin with those tasks that are only somewhat difficult (at the bottom of the hierarchy of fears you have drawn up). Remember, you already know that these particular assignments are *not* beyond you. You have been able to enter into these situations recently. What you need to do now is go just a little farther and stay just a little longer.

Although Perry was uneasy in any situation he could not extricate himself from immediately, the hierarchy of fears he drew up concerned itself mostly with his phobias for elevators and for driving. This is how it looked:

↑
INCREASING DIFFICULTY →
↓

10. Driving everywhere by myself.
9. Taking elevators to the top of the Empire State Building and taking rides in a friend's small airplane.
8. Driving to New York City by myself.
7. Driving to New York City with my wife.
6. Taking the same elevator at a time when there are no other people about.
5. Taking the elevator to the top of the courthouse when other people are also using it.
4. Driving by myself to a customer in the next town.
3. Driving my son to his school three miles away.
2. Driving by myself to the bridge tournament downtown and using the elevator to go up one flight.
1. Driving by myself through the neighborhood.

During the first week of treatment he pursued a more narrowly defined set of goals (a smaller hierarchy):

The first day he drove with a phobia aide one block past his usual perimeter. This was the most difficult day of the week. The prospect of going past the intersection that for over a year had bounded his ability to drive made him very anxious, although he knew he would be accompanied by someone else; but when the moment came, he was not really panicky. Each day he repeated this exercise with his wife. In addition, on the second day of treatment he drove by himself around his block, then each subsequent day a further block, except for one particular day when for no apparent reason he felt unable to go this extra distance. Also during that week he rode a familiar elevator, but only once and only one floor before getting off. Throughout these practice sessions he was concerned, as he usually was, that he might suddenly vomit, but the feeling of nausea was no worse than usual.

During this first week of practice, therefore, Perry made measurable progress but was still coping with those phobic situations that were least threatening. A few weeks later he was much further along. Throughout his treatment he had specific goals to reach every day and every week, with more long-range, more difficult goals to struggle toward in the future.

comforting to keep that thought in mind. The ordeal itself may be less of a problem than waiting for it. The first plane ride, usually the last phobic situation to be attacked, often has this character. The week of waiting, planning, and packing is worse than the flight itself.

Those among that larger group who do indeed have their worst moments in the phobic situation itself should keep in mind nevertheless that that awful turn of events they anticipate—being truly trapped somewhere, for example—rarely actually happens. The feelings of dread, of agitation, and of panic are only too likely to recur, unfortunately, but no new unprecedented catastrophe will follow in their wake. On those rare but inevitable occasions in life when a true emergency arises, phobics can be relied on to behave sensibly and effectively, no less than anyone else. In the face of a real crisis, imaginary fears are forgotten, only to return when the crisis is past.

There are finally those relatively few who have their worst moments after the trial. These are often people who misunderstand the phobic process and exposure therapy in particular. They think that if they did not quite manage to do everything they set out to do, or if they were especially anxious that day, they must necessarily be getting worse. Consequently, they are further shaken and depressed, and not infrequently reduced to tears. They can be comforted by coming to understand that these especially difficult days occur unpredictably but inevitably. They are not an indication of a worsening condition.

There are many reasons for carefully documenting your state of mind before, during, and after exposure to the phobic situation—but they sum to one principal reason: The pattern of your symptoms, although not identical from one time to the next, are likely to be similar. You will surely manage better each time if you know what to expect. For example, if you see time and again that your worst moments are directly *before* practicing, try to make that period of preparation and anticipation as brief as possible. If you find that the presence of a particular person puts you at ease, arrange to have him with you when you confront something especially difficult. If you notice that some peculiarity of setting—the weather, the shape or size of a classroom, some coincidence of diet—tends to worsen your symptoms, then take these into consideration when you are practicing. These details themselves constitute a phobia of a sort and require graduated exposure. If you recognize that over and over again you imagine a particular calamity that *never* happens, it will become easier as time goes on to turn your mind from these thoughts. To some extent, of course, it is precisely these thoughts that *cause* your anxiety. If you know that you are exhausted each time you practice more than an hour a day, practice somewhat less, or at least reserve time later on for some enjoyable, more relaxed activity. In general, you are interested in discovering those various things—activities, circumstances, thoughts—that reduce your level of anxiety somewhat and make it easier to enter further and remain longer in the phobic situation. As you proceed to do more and more, you should take inventory again since much of what is distressing now surely will not be later on, and occasionally what is at present comforting may not be later on.

3. Proceed step by step. Entering now into the phobic situation, with a new attitude—purposeful, determined— you should find yourself even at this early point in therapy doing more than you have been able to do in some time. This change in psychological set is by itself so powerful that some people look up after making their first efforts to find themselves further along than they had expected to be at the end of treatment! But they are the small minority. Most people have to proceed painfully from one task to another, and this is what you should begin to do now. Again making reference to the hierarchy of fears you have drawn up, do that task you judged to be only somewhat more difficult than the one you have just accomplished.

Then, as soon as you think you can manage it, attempt to do the next hardest, and so on. Do not wait until you feel comfortable somewhere before you venture further. Only when you are much further along does a particular place at last become comfortable.

Each new step should be planned ahead of time:

a. Decide where exactly you are going, with whom, and how long you are going to stay. As everyone knows, even the best laid plans tend to go awry—automobiles break down, trains are delayed, people do not arrive when they are supposed to. One of the things you should plan on, in fact, is what to do when something does go wrong. Phobics do not deal very well with the unexpected, and the fewer surprises the better. Your planning should include all those "what if" questions that come to mind and that otherwise impede any endeavor.

"What if the elevator gets stuck?"

"All right, what if the elevator gets stuck?"

"I'll scream, act crazy, have a heart attack, or fall down on the floor dead."

"Did you ever do any of those things before when you got panicky?"

"No."

"Well, then you won't do any of those things now, even if you do get trapped in an elevator and panicky."

"But what if the elevator gets stuck?"

All right. This is what you do if the elevator gets stuck. Keep in mind that you will *not* act crazy or do anything to embarrass yourself. There are people who do become hysterical in a stuck elevator, but they are rarely phobics. Phobics are too inhibited and self-conscious to let off steam that way. But suppose you do. Even someone who is hysterical calms down after a few minutes. No one will look down on you for crying and being very upset under such circumstances, and in any case no one will remember for very long just how you behaved. People stuck in an elevator are more interested in getting out than in carefully observing the other passengers. What they do—and what you will do if you are alone in the elevator—is what every sensible person does: First press some of the control buttons to see if the elevator starts, then press the emergency button or bang on the door until someone calls out to you. Many elevators have a telephone to call for help. Once you have made your presence known, all you have to do is wait. Waiting may be unpleasant for you, but it is not dangerous. Since waiting is indeed difficult, though, try to *do* something during that time. Talk to the other people in the elevator if there are any, or write down an account of your experience on whatever paper you find at hand. Or go over your checkbook. It doesn't matter what you do as long as you are doing something. You will be rescued almost always within ten to fifteen minutes. Those few who are trapped for much longer periods invariably calm down after the first fifteen or twenty minutes. Being stuck in an elevator is a boring if not benumbing experience.

"But what if the elevator gets stuck?"

It is as if the phobic's mind boggles at the question, returning to it again and again. Looming up before him is an unfathomable danger that resists rational planning. But if you are phobic, you must plan nevertheless.

If you are afraid, for example, of getting stuck in an elevator:

    i. Familiarize yourself with the control panel of that particular elevator and with its safety provisions.

    ii. Consider entering the first time accompanied by a friend.

    iii. Consider entering the next few times with a friend waiting for you outside.

iv. At a time when you will not disturb anyone, press the emergency button to see how loud the alarm is.

v. Bring along a pencil and notebook, or a book to read, or anything else likely to interest you over a period of time.

vi. Think of other things to do. Use your imagination in this way, not in the empty contemplation of disaster.

Similar strategies can be mapped out ahead of time for all those unlikely but conceivable dangers you may encounter. There are reasonable things to do if your car breaks down on a dark and stormy night and reasonable measures to take if you get lost in a dangerous neighborhood. But more important problems are likely to arise during a practice session. Certain things may go wrong when you become panicky, and these can surely be anticipated and planned for in a straightforward way. For example, if you think you may have to leave the practice session prematurely, you will feel more comfortable finding out ahead of time where all the exits are. Sometimes these are literally exits—from department stores, theaters, restaurants, or highways. More often they are simply ways out of particular situations, for instance having a ride home in case you have to leave a party early, or finding a shortcut in case a stretch of road proves too long. Most of the time you will not have to leave in the middle of a practice session, but knowing that it is possible to do so is reassuring and paradoxically makes it more likely you will be able to stay. Those times that you do leave, return to that situation as soon as you can. If you are standing in line and get so anxious you cannot stay a minute more, leave; but if possible, come back a few minutes later when you have calmed down. As in so many struggles in life, a failure at practicing becomes important only when it is not followed by a second attempt.

b. Have in mind a particular place you expect to be or distance you expect to travel, and plan to be there for a particular minimal period of time. Your purpose is to fulfill that plan, or go still farther, or stay still longer. But do not expect always to reach that goal.

There came a time in therapy when Theresa felt ready to attempt going into those quiet, dignified public places, such as libraries or churches, that had always seemed especially frightening to her. In such a setting she felt light-headed and likely to faint or make some kind of scene, such as getting up suddenly and running to the nearest exit. She had not been in such a place for years.

She began by going with a friend to a nearby bookstore which had somewhat the character of a library. This proved not as difficult as she had anticipated. Then she went by herself. Although she was bothered to some extent by her usual symptoms, they seemed less severe than usual, and she managed to remain five or six minutes before leaving. She returned to the store every day for the next few days. She then went by herself to a small neighborhood library. Immediately she was overcome by the rising sense of panic. Feeling defeated, she hurried out. She undertook this trial four days in a row and each time fared no better. Yet on the fifth day, for reasons that seemed obscure to her, she was *not* panicky. Glancing through a book of paintings by a favorite artist seemed to make her feel less nervous, and talking to the librarian helped. Altogether she remained for ten minutes with a tolerable level of anxiety. The following day when she returned, she felt comfortable. By the following week she was able to sit down and read, although still startled and upset from time to time by a sudden surge of panicky feelings.

Try to adhere to whatever goal you set for yourself each day. Keep in mind that today's practice session need not be much more difficult than yesterday's. Small advances—a few feet, a few seconds—are all that is required to guarantee recovery if they continue day after day.

c. After a week of practicing you should have some idea about how fast you can expect to progress, at least initially. On that basis, make a schedule of planned practice sessions for the following week. You should have specific goals. By the end of the week you may plan to stay alone at home for as long as a half hour or drive past an intersection a few miles away or visit a friend for coffee. The goal does not have to be very hard to reach. It need not be fulfilled, but you should have something concrete to strive for. At the end of that week you should list another set of goals for the following week. As time goes on you will want to set longer-range goals. A trip across country that once seemed unthinkable begins to seem possible. But modest expectations are appropriate at first. *Do not settle for going the same distance day after day.* Someone who is still practicing the same task after a month's trial, often with the thought that further progress has to wait for him to "get used" to what he is already doing, is not really practicing and will not get better. Some self-help groups, while preaching a philosophy of entering into the phobic situation, nevertheless tacitly encourage such a lack of progress by sympathetically reassuring the patient that he is "doing fine." Minimizing distress in this way only guarantees much more suffering over the long run. There are a few phobics who use these meetings and psychotherapy itself as an excuse for not practicing. Talking about their phobia becomes a substitute for doing something about it. This attitude will adversely affect the progress of others in the group. In such a case, it is altogether appropriate for a therapist or group leader, as a last resort, to ask that person not to attend these sessions for a while in order to bring home to him forcefully that talking is not enough. He can be allowed back into the group later. He must understand that it is sometimes necessary to attempt a new task before feeling quite ready to do so.

d. If you are about to go into a new situation—a party with people you do not know, a faraway vacation, a job interview, a college classroom—find out ahead of time as much as you can about that situation. The more you know, the more at ease you will feel and the better prepared you will be to deal not only with your anxieties but with the various real demands of that situation. Details are important. Knowing something about the people you expect to meet will make it easier to plan a conversation. Knowing how long it takes to arrive and to return home makes it possible to plan activities that will occupy your attention over that span of time. Knowing about the actual physical environment —the size and shape of the apartment or department store or beauty parlor—is helpful. If you think you may feel cramped in a particular place, you might want to plan on getting up every once in a while to go to the bathroom, make a telephone call, or simply pace. You may not choose to commit yourself to stay as long as you would otherwise. More important, when you know what to expect, you give less rein to your imagination. You won't worry about being trapped in an alcove if you know you are going to be at an outdoor barbecue. Similarly, minor complications won't grow to significant dimensions if they can be anticipated. For example, being kept waiting can be dreadful if it comes without warning, but if you know ahead of time that you may have to wait—and how long you may have to wait—it is usually manageable. As much as possible, do not be taken by surprise. Tell the people upon whom you depend not to confront you at the last minute with a change of plans.

e. Before engaging in an unusually threatening activity—for instance, addressing a group, taking an airplane ride, or even giving birth for the first time—

rehearse ahead of time what you will do, hour by hour, perhaps minute by minute. The better prepared you are, the more likely your success. Consult with others who have undertaken such a task. No situation demands complete passivity. There is always something you can do to affect your circumstances. Natural childbirth is founded on the principle that doing anything, including engaging in breathing exercises that have no effect on the process of birth, mitigates the pain and distress of labor. Similarly, there are things to do when waiting on line in a shopping center or standing on an escalator. While sitting in a dentist chair, when it is not possible to write, talk, or walk about, it is still possible to count off seconds on your fingers, time the panic on a wall clock, or figure the dimensions of the office. All of these activities serve to distract from the awful fantasy that is the panic attack. But it is necessary to know ahead of time how long you will be in the dentist's chair, what procedures will be done, and whether it will be possible, if you think it necessary, to stand up occasionally for a moment or two. And before you get to the dentist's office you should know something about how you are likely to react—how you will feel waiting for an appointment, driving to the office, sitting in the waiting room, and so on. You can learn by observing how you tolerate similar situations, and you can learn from others, for everyone's experience tends to be similar. The more you know about the situation you are going into and about your own reactions, the better.

If you venture to fly in an airplane for the first time you should expect this: the anxious moments begin long before the flight itself. When you first contemplate the idea of flying—weeks or months ahead of time—you will hesitate even to mention the possibility to your family, afraid they will become so eager that you will feel pressured into committing yourself prematurely. Either you will be forced to disappoint them, you may imagine, as probably you have done before, or be forced to drag yourself terrified onto the airplane. Consequently, you may have no one with whom to talk over your fears. You should begin, therefore, by explaining to your family that you are *not* committing yourself but that as part of the process of dealing with the fear of flying, you want to be able to speak to them and go over in your mind a *possible future* flight. Then you should consider where you *might* want to go and from what airport you *might* want to leave. The details of the trip are important. How early must you arrive at the airport? How is baggage handled? Will there be a baggage line? Is there a waiting area where friends can remain until the flight? Is there a point beyond which they cannot go? Is there a place to sit down, drink coffee, pace back and forth? How helpful are the attendants? Is it possible to get lost looking for the departure gate? What happens if you lose your boarding pass? Will you board through those movable tunnels or up a ladder? Will you be able to choose your seat? Will you feel more comfortable near a window or on the aisle? How long will you have to be strapped in? What happens if you take the seat belt off when you are not supposed to? Do the engines make a loud noise? Will the stewardesses give that upsetting lecture about life jackets? How many bathrooms are there on the airplane? Are you likely to have to wait to use them? How long does it take for the airplane to taxi to the runway? How long does it take before it gets underway, before it leaves the ground, before it banks, before it rises to cruising altitude, before you can remove your seat belt and walk about? And so on. You should find out if the trip is likely to be bumpy, how many people will be aboard, and if a movie will be shown. You should learn *anything* and *everything* that will make the experience of flying as specific and concrete as possible from beginning to end. During the days before the trip it is important to visualize these details and to plan for those moments when otherwise there would be nothing to do but wait. Waiting passively encourages flights of fancy. "What'll I do if the wing falls off?" "Suppose we hit an air pocket—whatever that is?" "Suppose I scream or lose control or whatever?" These are dreams only and require no answer, but the other questions posed above are important. Knowing the exact extent of a troublesome experience makes it easier to deal with. In particular, enforced periods of waiting should be anticipated. Different sorts of activities fill up different periods of time. In the airport you can make a telephone call. Later on while waiting to board you can talk to fellow passengers. A crossword puzzle may allow you to occupy yourself during the more prolonged idleness of sitting strapped in throughout takeoff.

More important, perhaps, is to prepare for the shifting but to some extent predictable changes of mood brought on by these various circumstances. In this regard, being prepared means simply knowing what to expect. The days and weeks before the airplane flight are marked by moments of anxiety when you remind yourself obsessively from time to time that the trip and the dangers you imagine are coming closer every day. These fears are ameliorated to an extent by planning and rehearsal only to erupt again a little while later. For many, these days are the worst part of the trip. The last day of packing and making final arrangements is particularly difficult because there is little chance to be distracted by other things. Sleep may come with difficulty that night, and then come the final hours. Intermittent thoughts of refusing to fly and making some last-minute excuse, however feeble and embarrassing, come to mind but are interrupted by the need to make last-minute practical arrangements for the trip. The anxiety seems especially sharp but is short-lived. Other bad times are the trip to the airport, waiting on line at the baggage counter, passing through the metal detector (the point of no return, it seems), and entering the traveler's lounge. Waiting in the lounge tends to be more difficult but still tolerable, especially if through therapy you have already become adept at lowering your level of anxiety.* By the time you climb aboard the aircraft, you are likely to be partly numb, partly still anxious, and, strangely, partly relaxed. Boarding, waiting for takeoff, and climbing to a cruising altitude are similarly trying, but if you have prepared properly —know what to expect and what to do—the trip itself is usually anticlimactic, not miserable if not exactly comfortable.

This is the average experience. Certainly there are some who have a harder time. Occasionally someone sits immobile, squeezing the arms of his chair throughout the entire trip, but no one loses control or behaves outrageously. More commonly the difficult times I have described prove not to be so difficult just because their dangers, such as they are, are foreseen. Some people arrive exhausted, but many are exhilarated, having conquered an irrational fear that may have bedeviled them over the course of a lifetime. No one arrives terrified. No one regrets having invested so much time and trouble.

It would be nice to think that one such victory conquers the phobia, but neither the fear of flying nor any other fear disappears so readily. A second flight is likely to be more comfortable, but not necessarily. Only after many flights and only when you feel confident that you have learned the techniques for reliably lowering your levels of anxiety does the phobia disappear once and for all.

4. Every success should be recapitulated: reviewed subsequently and repeated as soon as possible. These include

* See the next chapter.

the signal victories such as the first airplane flight, but also the lesser yet probably more important accomplishments of daily practicing. *It is by these experiences rather than by classroom indoctrination that phobic thinking changes. Not by an act of faith does one begin to have confidence in his ability to overcome his phobia but by seeing it happen.* Just as your phobia is sustained by the memory of all those times you were panicky and ran away, it is undermined by the memory of those times you did not run away. When these newer, happier memories begin to predominate, the expectations you have when entering a phobic situation change. You expect to be able to remain, and as a consequence you can. In a sense, it is only the memory of being phobic that makes you phobic, so it is important to underline every success. Keep track of those moments when you were able to cross the threshold of a difficult place even though you thought you could not; when you thought you were trapped, and an unexpected exit appeared before you; when you thought you could not stay another moment, yet you were able to do so; when you thought the panic was spiraling uncontrollably, and yet by doing some particular thing you were able to lower your level of anxiety. Yesterday's success, fresh in mind, outweighs a great many previous failures. A row of such successes builds quickly each upon the next, "locking in" improvement. So much is true of any learning process. An activity that is difficult and uncertain at first and that requires great attention becomes effortless with practice. The more practice, the better. The longer the practice sessions, the better. The closer together they are, the better.

5. If you find a practice session is accomplished easily, consider extending the trial. It is not necessary to practice to the point of exhaustion; neither is it necessary to suffer every day. On the other hand, nothing will be lost by venturing "too far."

Perry worked persistently to defeat his driving phobia, practicing each day by driving a little farther than the day before, sometimes accompanied by his wife, sometimes alone. He drove even on those days when he thought he would not be able to drive at all. There came a particular day, though, when Perry turned the car the wrong way and headed down a long detour. As he traveled farther and farther from familiar territory, he became more and more anxious, although not quite panicky. He grabbed hold of the wheel so tightly his arms began to tremble, and his foot shook on the accelerator. His mouth became very dry. He noticed his heart beating "too fast." Troubling him even more than these physical symptoms was the thought that, however accustomed, he might lose control of himself or of the car. He drove in this agitated state for fifteen minutes before finding his way back to familiar neighborhoods. By then he felt distracted and exhausted. He was unable to do any work the rest of the day. But he also felt a certain exhilaration at having driven a greater distance than he ever had before. It was, nevertheless, another week before he could force himself to drive that difficult route again.

Would Perry have managed to get well without putting himself through the special turmoil of his trip? Certainly. As determined as he was, systematically practicing every day, he would have conquered his phobia in the end. Did he get better faster by pushing himself this extra distance? Probably, but not necessarily. No single experience weighs heavily in the outcome of therapy. Did this especially painful experience slow his recovery? Certainly not. It would have if he had been deterred from venturing forth the next day. Someone who understands what needs to be done to get well will not be put off by an exhausting but not dangerous experience.

6. Do not expect one success to be followed unfailingly by another. Even when therapy proceeds as smoothly as possible, there are setbacks. But make sure you understand what a setback is. An especially painful or prolonged panic

attack is *not* a failure of therapy. Neither is the inability to do as much on a particular practice session as you would have liked. Both of these are inevitable from time to time and consistent with steady improvement. Running away from a place *at the first moment of getting panicky* is a failure. It is the only failure other than the more profound failure of not trying to get better in the first place. A setback is being unable to go to some place previously accessible to you or to remain there. Failures and setbacks are not inevitable, but they are so common as to be the rule. Fortunately, the final outcome of treatment is not threatened by these difficulties along the way *unless you become disheartened.* An inability to tolerate the phobic situation a few days in a row does not invariably presage difficulty for the following day. Sometimes, just as a panic attack occurs inexplicably, so do moments of complete calm. In any case, a slow, steadfast reentry into the phobic situation will once again make it manageable, and further improvement can follow readily. One setback does not imply that there will be others, but even with repeated setbacks, final, complete recovery is still possible *as long as you keep trying.*

7. Plan each day how far into the phobic situation you will go, but know that there will be times when you will not be able to accomplish all you set out to do. These sessions are useful anyway. Best of all are those times when you exceed your expectations, going beyond what you thought was possible. These triumphs come either because you are relatively at ease on a particular day for no particular reason, or when you are emboldened by having just overcome an especially difficult phobic situation. Next best is to do what you set out to do, whether you become panicky or not, *but going only partway is still a success.* In the long run, all that is required to overcome the phobia is going each day just a little bit further into the phobic situation and staying just a little bit longer.

Because of her phobia, Janet had refused for years to attend any social gatherings. Of special importance among these was the annual party given by her husband's employer. After beginning treatment she found that some social occasions had become tolerable, and so, to her husband's surprise, she agreed to attend that year's party. She bought a dress and arranged for a baby-sitter. More important, she called to say they were coming. When the evening arrived, she felt very anxious. Nevertheless, she dressed, picked up the baby-sitter, and followed through on all the arrangements she had previously made. With growing uneasiness she sat quietly in the car throughout the short trip to the hotel where the party was held. She got as far as the lobby, but when she heard the music and the hubbub of all the people talking and laughing, she suddenly felt she had to turn back. Her husband made an excuse, and they left. She cried all the way home because, as she put it, she had "failed again."

But she had not failed. She had taken an important first step. Had she managed only to *make preparations* for going to the party, she still would have been making progress. The further she could get the better, but only an unwillingness to entertain the possibility of going should have been regarded as an unequivocal failure. Even getting into the car and promptly getting out again would have been satisfactory. There is no shame in starting and stopping. Someone who feels that every plan he makes must be executed exactly will be afraid of making ambitious plans and soon will not want to practice at all. It is the disappointment some people feel going only partway that prejudices their ultimate recovery. They expect too much and get discouraged too soon. Very often someone who thinks he cannot confront a particular situation but who is willing to try—even to begin to try—finds that once he has begun, carrying through to the end is not difficult.

Going to the place where the party was held was a necessary first step for Janet to going to the party itself. It was not the last time she got up to a place without going in. These limited excursions made a contribution to her being able to attend comfortably her husband's annual business party when it was held again the following year.

8. Do not look for excuses to avoid practicing. There are times, of course, when you may be too ill or too busy—the world contrives circumstances to which we must accommodate ourselves no matter what our priorities—but when you have a cold, or when you are worn out from work, or disturbed by a family argument, practice anyway. Do not wait until you are "feeling up to it." You need to demonstrate to yourself that you can function in the phobic situation *no matter how you feel*. Phobics relate their state of mind and their ability to function to all sorts of extraneous conditions, including not only the weather, the time of day, and the clothes they are wearing but also internal states: hunger, sleepiness, or any sort of physical distress. Because they believe in these connections, the connections become real. The fact is, although uncomfortable, phobics can manage these minor discomforts as well as anyone else. Since these irrational associations become part of the greater fear that is the phobia itself, they must be treated in the same way. If you can go a certain distance when you are rested, you may reasonably plan on going more slowly or for a shorter distance when you are tired—but do not skip practicing altogether. Above all, *do not tell yourself there is no time in your schedule for practicing!* The time required is very small, and getting well is really important.

9. When you are approaching a difficult phobic situation for the first time, use any crutch that is likely to help.

Perry found for a period of time that he could only drive places by having paper and pencil with him to write letters.

At first Theresa could not enter a bookstore without having a friend along.

Another patient carried a can of soda with her everywhere in case she should "choke."

Someone else would drive only if the car was equipped with a CB radio "for emergencies."

The idea of using a crutch is distasteful to some people, seeming to encourage a new dependence in someone who is already overly dependent on props or on other people. Having to take medication or hold on magically to a helper or to a list of things to do seems unwarranted when all that needs to be confronted is a feeling. But it is a terrible feeling. Particularly painful are those moments when a new task is being attempted. Whatever makes that task easier is justified. A psychological crutch used properly functions similar to a real crutch—it helps someone who is impaired do more than he otherwise could and is discarded as soon as he can manage without it. Crutches can be used *improperly* in a number of different ways:

a. A crutch should not be offered to someone who does not need it. A person who has a weak leg muscle, for example, should not rely indefinitely on a crutch to get around or his muscle will get still weaker rather than stronger. Similarly, a phobic who can struggle with difficulty to walk by himself to the corner grocery store should not ask someone to accompany him *simply in order to feel more comfortable*, except perhaps very occasionally. If he does, sooner or later he will be *unable* to go there by himself, no matter how hard he struggles. One patient, a phobic woman who always imagined that she was about to fall to the ground, was offered a cane by her therapist "in order to feel more secure," with the result that she was soon unable to go anywhere without the cane.

b. A crutch should not suggest to the user that he has a weakness or deficiency that in fact he does not have. Someone given a crutch to use because of a broken leg —when he does not have a broken leg—will suffer unnecessary concern and be led away from the proper treatment of his condition, whatever it may be. It is one thing for a phobic to drink a soda, for example, to distract himself from a phobic situation, knowing the soda serves only that purpose,* but it is quite another to imagine the soda has an ingredient, such as sugar, that relieves some psychological abnormality. The phobic has enough to worry about without thinking he has an obscure physical malady.

c. A crutch should be used only temporarily, just long enough for the individual to become strong enough to do without it. Used for an unnecessarily long period of time, a crutch delays rather than facilitates recovery. The goal of treatment, after all, is to be able to go anywhere and do anything anybody else can do without special accommodation. Putting aside the crutch, when the time finally comes, is always difficult. As in so much else in the treatment of phobias, it is often necessary to do this difficult thing before one feels quite ready to do it.

The Helper

A very special aid or crutch is the helper. The purpose he serves and the manner in which he should fulfill his role are discussed in Chapter 7. The way in which you should work with him is described below.

a. Listen to him. You do not have to agree with him. He may not be right. Indeed, he cannot be right all the time. If he knows you pretty well and thinks you can do a particular thing on a particular day, he may still be wrong. You are the final judge of what you can or cannot do. But he is not likely to be wrong. Observing you objectively day after day he may know more about you than you do yourself.

b. If he has a particular suggestion on how to deal with a phobic situation or the panic itself, give it a try. He may have noticed that you handle stresses better one

---

* See the next chapter.

way than another or that you calm down more reliably by doing one thing rather than another. You may have been too caught up with the anxieties of the moment to observe yourself accurately. If he is a trained phobia aide, he will know from previous experience with other patients what is likely to work. Especially important are ways for dealing with the "stuck points" that come up inevitably along the way of recovery. What has helped others is likely to help you.

c. Those circumstances that are especially frightening should be confronted for the first time with a helper if possible. After a while the helper should be at a distance, then as time goes on farther and farther away, until he is out of sight if not out of reach.

Of all the public places Theresa had avoided for years, the most threatening was the great public library at the center of the city. The crowds of people walking together down the long hallways, the greater number sitting quietly in the cavernous reading room, the atmosphere itself, somber and silent and serious, all worked to unnerve her. "What if I start yelling suddenly?" she thought; and the thought seemed to make the possibility of her becoming hysterical more real. When smaller libraries had at last become accessible to her, this most imposing, most intimidating place was still outside her phobic boundaries. Overcoming this last barrier required a special effort, and it began with her consulting and making plans with her helper. That was the first step.

Step 2: Continuing these conversations while sitting on the stone steps of the library.

Step 3: Walking together through the entranceway into the great central hall. Standing there until her level of anxiety receded.

Step 4: Standing apart at opposite ends of the hall although within sight of each other.

Step 5: Walking together through the building.

Step 6: Sitting together in the main reading room.

Step 7: Sitting apart at the same table, then at different tables, then at opposite sides of the room.

Step 8: Separating. While her helper waited at a specific place, the front desk, Theresa walked tentatively along the hallways and into the various rooms. For a short period she sat by herself in the main reading room.

Step 9: The last step: With her helper remaining at home where she could be reached by telephone, Theresa returned to the library two more times. But she had to return many more times entirely by herself and spend much more time in the library before she felt truly comfortable.

Perhaps in certain ways a helper may be with you always, no farther away than the other end of a telephone. In that peculiar sense no one is ever alone. No one ever achieves greater independence. There is no such thing. No one, no matter how unafraid, can live entirely apart from everyone else.

10. Keep in mind these further principles:

a. The difficult effort required to enter into a phobic situation is made easier if you can engage in a pleasurable activity. In other words, going into a movie theater may be threatening but less painful in the end *if you like movies.* The movie itself becomes a reason to attend over and above the primary purpose of learning how to overcome your fear. Arranging rewards, therefore, is helpful. If you must practice entering into a restaurant, choose a nice restaurant. If you must drive a distance, try to visit a friend whose company you enjoy. Unmitigatedly painful excursions will be necessary from time to time, but the less painful the better.

b. One prolonged practice session is better than two shorter sessions. There is more time to adjust and more time, consequently, to experience a particular phobic situation without anxiety—and subsequently to remember it that way. Very brief practice sessions hardly help at all. Someone may use an elevator every day for years without overcoming his fear of elevators. The ride, lasting only a few seconds, gives little opportunity to practice lowering the level of anxiety by conscious effort, and still less time for it to go away by itself. Conversely, someone stuck in an elevator for an hour will calm down long before his release.

c. If you have to confront an especially difficult task on the weekend, make sure you practice the previous week. Waiting for the weekend to come will be less upsetting. It is as if the phobic can only worry so much and no more. Anticipating tomorrow's difficulties gets in the way of worrying about the weekend. This is one more example of controlling your thoughts by first controlling your behavior.

d. *While you are getting better in some ways, do not get worse in others!* While you are practicing, and consequently entering more and more into situations you have previously avoided, do not allow yourself to start withdrawing from situations which up to now you have found tolerable. As the phobic process can be reversed, leading to recovery, so can the process of recovery be reversed, leading to a relapse or to a worsening of the phobia. In such a way new phobias can appear throughout the course of an agoraphobia. But it is at that moment when for the first time you are tempted to avoid a particular place that by an effort of will alone you can overcome your fear. Once avoidance of a particular place has developed into a pattern, overcoming your fear of that place becomes much more difficult.

In summary: Progress in this stage is marked by a slowly enhanced ability to confront and remain in phobic circumstances. Barely perceptible progress becomes more obvious with repeated practice sessions, becoming steadily more accelerated until each phobic situation, one after the other, loses its ability to terrify. It would be nice to say that the force of the panic attack is lessened along the way, but such is not the case. There comes a time when certain areas become relatively comfortable, but in those more difficult circumstances that you have not yet mastered, panic attacks may still occur regularly, as they may occur occasionally anywhere. And the physical symptoms seem just as bad. And the sense of losing control, unfortunately, seems also just as bad. The problems of this stage of treatment, therefore, overlap with those of the next: learning how to manage the panic itself.

FEELINGS TO COPE WITH AT THIS STAGE: impatience and fatigue.

Chapter 5

STAGE FIVE: TOLERATING DISTRESS

Most phobics expect that treatment will work to make them progressively less and less anxious, allowing them as time goes on to enter comfortably into phobic circumstances that previously made them panicky. The real situation is more complicated. Progress is judged by what the phobic can do and not how he feels. Initially, since he will be entering into more and more difficult circumstances, he may even feel worse. When treatment is advanced, it is true, the panic attacks become less frequent and shorter in duration. There are indeed more and more areas in which the phobic feels no distress, but until the very end of treatment he will, unpredictably, become panicky again. There is no way to get better—to relearn those mistakes in learning that led to the phobia in the first place—without being at least somewhat anxious in every phobic practice session and often panicky. It is certainly not possible to get better once and for all without ever getting panicky.

A man flew from the Midwest where he lived to White Plains with the single purpose of attending the phobia clinic and overcoming his driving phobia. He immediately threw himself wholeheartedly into the business of practicing. In only a matter of days he was driving everywhere in the vicinity *without any anxiety at all!* In fact, throughout his entire stay he never once had a panic attack, no matter where he drove or whatever the circumstances, despite being instructed to *try* to get panicky. He finally returned home thinking he had conquered his fear once and for all, only to be immobilized once again by a panic attack that struck within the first few days of his driving through familiar neighborhoods. He had learned "the theory" but had not learned how to manage his panicky feelings, and sooner or later they were bound to return.

A woman who had the single fear of driving in the rain attended each of the first six weeks of a phobia clinic. She was encouraged by the progress of everyone in the group and felt that by observing them she had learned the principles of exposure therapy. For the first time in her life she felt she could drive anywhere without being deterred by a distant cloud in the sky. But during those six weeks it had not yet rained, and when finally she was caught driving in the rain, that same sick feeling that had paralyzed her so many times before rendered her helpless once again. It was only after she had practiced many times driving in the rain and had coped many times with these bad feelings *when they were at their most extreme* that she finally overcame her phobia.

During this stage the phobic must learn to tolerate distress and learn methods for lessening the level of anxiety to tolerable proportions. These techniques are very important! It is probably possible to overcome a phobia by brute force alone. Someone who stubbornly refuses to avoid a particular situation, no matter how awful he feels, will ultimately lose his fear of those feelings and that place. Someone so indomitable, however, probably would never have become phobic in the first place. For most, the awful feelings brought on by the phobic situation seem intolerable. A strategy of brute force is not possible for them. They need to find ways to lower their level of anxiety, if only just a little, and only just for a while. With repeated practice these techniques become more and more effective, controlling the anxiety more reliably and to a greater and greater extent until it becomes possible to switch off the panicky feelings altogether! The goal of this stage of treatment is to systematically persevere until this truth, unbelievable to every phobic at the beginning of treatment, becomes evident.

INSTRUCTIONS

1. Remember, first of all, that the panic attack cannot hurt you. It cannot drive you mad. The physiological response it engenders is part of the "fight or flight" reaction and is not destructive to the body, even when it occurs over and over again. Recognition of this fact is crucial to the progress of exposure therapy. But how can one be sure? It is known that people die suddenly under all sorts of circumstances, sometimes inexplicably, and there are people, some people at least, who seemingly without warning become psychotic. Why is it not possible that some especially terrible panic attack might prove fatal some day or, if not quite so deadly, why could it not lead to an irreversible disorganization of personality?

From a certain philosophical point of view it may be said that no one can know anything for sure. Unprecedented events do occur. But if any such extraordinary event were actually to grow out of a panic attack, it would be just that—extraordinary and without precedent. Thousands of patients have been seen in phobia clinics. Most of them have been panicky a great many times, often hundreds of times, and to the best of my knowledge no such thing has been reported. This is certainly true for the hundreds of patients I myself have seen. No one has choked, convulsed, suffered a heart attack or psychotic break, developed amnesia, attacked anyone, acted wild, or fallen to the ground dead. It is as if the panic attack can only go so far and no further. If human beings were immobilized or fell apart physically in the face of overwhelming fear, the race would have died out long ago. Can you imagine a caveman responding to a saber-toothed tiger by falling to the ground with a heart attack or running around out of control? But is it not conceivable, a phobic is likely to ask, that he himself may prove the first exception? To that question there is no sensible answer. If some day I hear of a phobic person who suffered a heart attack during a panic attack, I would regard it as a coincidence. It would be too remarkable an event, the connection too tenuous, to explain it through cause and effect. After all, people have heart attacks during their sleep without anyone concluding that sleep is dangerous.

Unfortunately, no one who has been phobic for any length of time takes these assurances at face value. You may feel that you have good reason to think otherwise. Therefore, you must discover the truth for yourself. When you see finally that the panic attack is not inherently dangerous, you will have achieved the principal goal of treatment. The panic attack—*which remains to the end a very unpleasant feeling*—loses its ability to terrify.

2. Remember also that future panic attacks are not likely to be worse than those you have experienced in the past. This also is hard to believe. It seems that each attack is on the verge of spiraling out of all control and is stopped from getting worse only by a stroke of luck or by running away that very moment. In reality the panic attack can only get so bad and no worse. If you want to know what is likely to happen to you should you get panicky in new, more difficult circumstances, ask yourself what happened in the past. Did you injure yourself in any way? Did you behave recklessly? Did you really lose control of yourself, scream, or act crazy? Did you faint? Were you incapacitated, or did it only seem so? Did you really embarrass yourself—judged not by the unreasonable standards of the typical phobic but by the people around you? If the answers are no, then you need not worry that you will do any of these things in the future. What you are likely to do is what you have done in the past: fall abruptly silent, look suddenly preoccupied or

possibly distressed, inclined to stop whatever you are doing and leave. And you are likely to feel terrible. But nothing worse.

3. Expect the panicky feelings to come.

Once Janet understood that she had a condition called agoraphobia and that it was not hopeless, she threw herself into treatment. Working stubbornly every day, she was soon able to go places she had not been for years. She noticed a somewhat heightened level of anxiety during these first days and weeks of venturing into restaurants and beauty parlors, but she was not panicky more often than usual. She had panic attacks, sometimes two or three days in a row, only to be free of them completely the following week. She could find no particular reason to explain why she should feel overcome in such a way on certain occasions and not others, but she was not especially taken aback because this had always been the case. As she improved in succeeding weeks, her panic attacks became more infrequent—once at a fancy restaurant, a couple of times, not surprisingly, at libraries, and once while taking a shower at a friend's house. Those she experienced in the library she attributed to the memory of all those previous times she had become panicky in that silent and oppressive setting. The time she was suddenly very anxious in the restaurant, she realized, was probably because the person sitting across from her had begun telling a story about a man who had suddenly started screaming in a department store. This fanciful anecdote touched too closely on her own fears of losing control. But she was puzzled by becoming so suddenly agitated while showering in a secure and familiar setting. She had visited her friend and showered there many times before without feeling any distress at all. Then she remembered that a moment before she had noticed she was beginning to gain weight. A chain of associations went through her mind so quickly that she was barely able only a few minutes later to reconstruct the connections. The thought that she might be getting fat had reminded her of her mother's family, all of whom were fat, and particularly her uncle who had been told he would have to lose considerable weight in order to avoid a heart attack. And then with graphic clarity she pictured herself struck down by a heart attack, lying helpless in bed in a cardiac care unit, her family gathered around, a priest intoning last rites. No wonder a moment later she was panicky! No more was required to precipitate an attack.

This pattern is typical. Panic attacks occur seemingly randomly throughout treatment, although less frequently toward the end. It would be nice to know just why they happen when they do, whether in reaction to an unwanted, perhaps unconscious idea, as seemed to be true at least some of the time in Janet's case, or, as one of her doctors thought, out of an inborn peculiarity of physiological response. By that account a phobic may become panicky under stress, just as someone else might develop a headache or stomach cramps. But it is not necessary to settle this theoretical question before engaging successfully in treatment. Whatever the cause, the phobic must come to expect the occasional return of these attacks because they do indeed recur, sometimes over a period of days only to disappear then for months. Their appearance should not be construed as a failure of treatment. In short, do not be disappointed by the inevitable. Be prepared. Remember: You may not be able to prevent the panic attack from coming, but with proper training you can make it go away.

4. As you keep track of your anxiety in general, keep particular track of your panic attacks: when they occur, how long they last, what makes them go away. You may find they are provoked by a particular external set of circumstances: waiting at a street corner, visiting relatives, driving at night, and so on. The more you know about these circumstances, the better you can prepare. Part of the dismay generated by an attack comes from its being unexpected. Monitor your thoughts also. If you get panicky mostly at times when you try not to be angry, you should make a special effort to express those feelings openly. Fatigue may stimulate an attack, as might any other particular state of mind. Most important of all, *time* your attacks. They usually last only a minute or two at their worst, although occasionally they may hover for hours between that

extreme and a level only slightly less severe. Still, if you find they are severe each time for only a minute, you will find coping with them much easier. The sense of spiraling, ever-increasing fear will be seen to be an illusion. Certain other aspects of the panic attack become apparent when it is observed systematically:

Minor overt physical changes do occur, but these are rarely apparent to other people. They include sweating palms and trembling. Some people blush.* Some breathe deeply. Phobics tend to be inordinately ashamed of these symptoms, attributing a significance to them that completely escapes everyone else. They may avoid places and people simply out of a fear of revealing whatever weakness or failing they think these overt physical signs represent. The unsteadiness, "dizziness," weakness, and other subjective complaints phobics report are not visible at all. Neither do these unpleasant feelings interfere seriously with walking, driving a car, or other such largely automatic activities. Activities that require concentration, such as studying for an examination, will suffer. However, when concentration and prompt appropriate action are urgent, as in an emergency, the panic attack fades immediately.

Although panic attacks tend to recur in similar circumstances, they will not do so invariably. Sometimes, for no apparent reason, someone will feel comfortable in a situation ordinarily threatening to him. Similarly, at times he will suffer a panic attack in places where he always felt safe. They may occur intermittently anywhere. Situations that require waiting passively, such as sitting under a hairdryer, are particularly likely to stimulate an attack. *In general, when an attack comes very suddenly and spikes to a very high level, it will also recede quickly.* Most uncomfortable of all are those uncommon occasions, usually when the phobic feels trapped somewhere, when the panic

---

* The fear of blushing, erythrophobia, is usually accompanied by the idea that the blushing is so extreme it causes others to become uncomfortable and blush! This idea may assume delusional proportions and is often intractable.

attacks, although still brief, return every few minutes over a period as long as an hour or more. These episodes can be demoralizing, but they are no more dangerous and are no more suggestive of a failure in therapy than occasional isolated attacks.

5. Prepare for anxious feelings and for the panic attack itself just as you prepare for the threatening circumstances of the phobic situation. There is one key to managing the panic attack, and it is perhaps the fundamental principle of treatment: Do not wait passively for the sense of rising danger and growing helplessness to engulf you. Do something! Become active. Assert control of yourself by acting upon your environment. By acting purposefully, you take hold of your thoughts and feelings. The panic attack distracts you from the business of life that would ordinarily occupy your attention. You must train yourself now to distract yourself from the preoccupation that is the panic attack. This facility does not come easily. The very word "panic" suggests an inability to think or act in control, but such is not the case. Like any other strong feeling, the expression of fear can be modified and controlled. Indeed, people can be trained to face calmly the most extreme danger—real, life-threatening danger, as opposed to the imaginary dangers of the panic attack. However, there should be no underestimating the force of this emotional reaction. It is changed very slowly and only after considerable training. The tools suggested below work but only after long hours of practice. Once again, the fundamental idea underlying all of these suggestions is: Be active in thought and behavior. The more your attention is turned away from your anxiety, the less severe it becomes. There comes a time when you can make it go away entirely.

Have ready, appropriate to each phobic situation, a list of things to do in order to distract yourself from the sense of spiraling fear. For example, if you feel anxious waiting on line in a supermarket:

- Keep records in a notebook of the fluctuations in your anxiety, minute by minute.
- Talk to the person in front of you—about anything.
- Add up in your mind the prices of the purchases you wish to make.
- Time how long it takes each person to get to the head of the line.
- Balance your checkbook.
- Unwrap and chew gum.
- Count the number of people in the store.
- Feel the texture of a fruit or vegetable.
- Write a letter.

And so on. Have similar lists for staying at home alone, riding escalators, flying in an airplane, sitting in a barbershop, riding in a train, sitting through a formal dinner, walking on a beach or on the top floor of an open garage, making your way through a department store, driving across a bridge, coping with someone's pet, or sitting in a classroom. In short, make a list for dealing with any phobic situation that must be endured for more than a few minutes at a time.

These plans should be marked down in detail on a piece of paper that can be held *in the hand*. Otherwise, at least in the beginning of therapy, you will not be able to remember them. At the moment of panic every idea and good intention flies out of mind, leaving only those accustomed thoughts of imminent danger and the need for flight. Holding the piece of paper concretely in hand makes it easier to focus on these tasks. The mere act of reading through the list is helpful. If the recommendations at the top of the list do not work, as they probably will not initially, try the others. *Remember, the panic attack does not last very long in any case.* By the time you get to the bottom of the list —if only you can wait long enough—the panic attack is likely to be subsiding. As one might expect, these techniques work more reliably on those occasions when someone is only moderately anxious, not quite panicky. Happily, in most phobic circumstances, even going further and further into the phobic situation, you will be at this less severe level of anxiety. Although surely somewhat anxious most of the time you practice—indeed, if you are not, you are probably not really practicing—if you are typical you will be truly panicky only every once in a while. At one extreme, a few report panic attacks once or twice a day, usually only for a few days in a row. A greater number report attacks no more than once every week or so, or even less frequently. There are some who, having begun treatment, have trouble getting panicky! It is as if by *wanting* to get panicky in order to practice these methods of dealing with the feeling, they are no longer able to! That active posture prevents the sense of helplessness which is integral to the phobic process. One example is the man who came here from the Midwest for treatment of his driving phobia only to find himself driving comfortably everywhere. It is quite exceptional for someone who has been panicky intermittently for years to suddenly lose the capacity to react in such a way, but when it does happen, it creates a problem in treatment. In order to get well it is necessary for the phobic to lose his fear of becoming panicky. In order to lose his fear he has to get panicky often enough—in controlled circumstances—to come to understand that there is, in fact, nothing to be afraid of, that with proper training he can manage his feelings and his behavior. Were there really a medication that could be relied on to block panic attacks, it would still fall short of this goal. What would happen after the medication was stopped? Should the panic attacks return, the phobic would once again have to go back on the drug, or, more likely, judging from the way the minor tranquilizers are used, simply take it indefinitely.

The ideas listed above for dealing with anxiety can be

expanded indefinitely.* They divide into two main categories:

   a. *Tools of rote:* Those that are easy to use but work only moderately well. These are simple rote activities directed at keeping the individual focused on the present. They work by distracting from "what if" thinking and other flights of fantasy. Because they require so little attention, however, they serve for only a moment at a time to distract from the overwhelming impact of a panic attack. Examples relevant to the situation of waiting in line at a supermarket include:

   i. *Looking attentively at things:* the design on a cereal box, magazine covers, the shape and colors of vegetables, the pattern of the floor tiles, the lighting, traffic visible through the windows, and people doing all the various intricate things they do.

   ii. *Listening attentively:* background noises, the rhythm of the cash register, random conversation, the ticking of a clock.

   iii. *Feeling things:* besides vegetables, the ribbing of the cart, the texture of a bit of cloth, the chewing-gum wrapper, a rubber band tied around your wrist, a safety pin, the sharp edge of keys, a comb, and so on.

   iv. *Tasting or smelling things:* candy, crackers, perfume, burnt matches, cigarettes, and so on.

   v. *Engaging in repetitive acts:* counting things, tapping fingers or feet, rolling and unrolling pieces of paper, whistling, reciting phrases,† or engaging in other such purely mechanical behaviors.

---

* See the Appendix.

† It does not matter what the phrase is. Some people repeat to themselves over and over a doctor's assurance that they will be all right. Some pray. Some tell themselves, "I'm relaxing my body. I'm relaxing my mind." Others recite a mantra or other nonsensical phrases. In this context, none of these words have content. It is the saying of them that is helpful.

As can be grasped readily, a similar list can be drawn up for every conceivable phobic situation. Someone driving a car, for instance, may not have a vegetable at hand to feel and admire, but he can twiddle the radio dials, count the bumps on the steering wheel, or keep track of the changing scenery. None of these tools is preferable to the others, which is another way of saying that what works for one person may not work for someone else. Effectiveness depends not on any particular aspect of the various rote behaviors but on when they are introduced in therapy. Those attempted first are not likely to work well because they are tried when the phobic is still very frightened and skeptical. New to the idea of trying to take control of his anxious feelings, he runs his fingers down such a list of suggestions only halfheartedly trying one before hurrying nervously on to the next. Even these first feeble attempts are a victory since they interrupt the otherwise automatic pattern of spiraling fear and immediate flight. By the time the phobic notices that his level of anxiety has indeed dropped somewhat, he is likely to have reached the middle of the list. So whatever he happens to have marked down at that point is what works. And with practice it works better and better, more effectively and more reliably.

b. *Tools of concentration:* Those that work well but are difficult to do, especially at the beginning of treatment. These are activities that require the phobic's attention. The more they command that attention, the more effective they are. On the other hand, since they demand that the phobic concentrate in order to perform them, he may not be able to engage in them at all when he is very anxious. Consider balancing one's checkbook. Someone who can concentrate on the necessary calculations even for a little while can distract himself from the panic attack long enough for his levels of anxiety to recede, but someone truly panicky is going to have great difficulty doing these calculations. The fact is that such tasks which seem at first glance to be impossible are accomplished in the end after considerable practice. The harder they are, the more practice they require. On the list of such tools mentioned above appropriate to waiting on line at a supermarket, those that are tools of concentration include:

· Talking to other people.
· Adding or subtracting prices or other figures.
· Timing events.
· Writing a letter.

These and all other tools of concentration fall into a few major categories:

i. Interactions with other people. Conversation with a helper, friends, even strangers is an accustomed yet powerful distraction. Talking is better than listening since it is more active, but the interaction is what is important. Having to respond to others focuses one's attention on something other than the anxious or panicky feelings. Some sort of conversation is possible almost anywhere. Someone waiting on line can speak to the person in front of him or behind him. When alone in a department store he can speak to a clerk. When driving by himself in an automobile, he can use a CB radio to find someone to talk to. At home alone there is the telephone. Even in an elevator it is possible to make small talk. The more compelling the subject of the conversation, the more involved the phobic will be and the less preoccupied he will be with himself. Strong expressions of feeling may have a cathartic effect, directly lowering the level of anxiety. Arguing may work best. Humor too serves very well to distract, but when someone is very anxious it is probably easier to pick a fight than to be funny. Transactions between people require concentration.

These include not only business transactions, such as purchases, but mutual plans and other sorts of arrangements—getting a telephone number from information, asking directions or the price of something, making any sort of request or expressing an opinion. In the final analysis, the mere act of talking itself is helpful.

ii. Writing. This requires thought and tends to crowd out other more unpleasant thoughts. Carrying around a small notebook is suitable for this purpose. When phobics are anxious they may write in it about whatever subject they choose. Some people keep a diary. Others make out a schedule for that day or for the coming week. Some produce long lists of random subjects—musical comedies or books by Russian authors. What they write should be interesting to them but does not have to make much sense. Record keeping is an effective way of focusing a phobic's thoughts on something other than his own anxious feelings—even if what he is recording are his own feelings!* It would seem that standing apart from oneself psychologically just far enough to observe rather than simply react is enough to alter the experience. The immediacy and the *urgency* of the panic attack recede—although, once again, only a little at the beginning of treatment and only for a moment. The more involved the phobic becomes in this process of note-taking, the more control he develops over his anxiety. If he can become *engrossed* in what he is writing, his anxiety will disappear altogether.

iii. Calculations. Figuring requires concentration. The worse someone is at it, the more concentration it requires. The sorts of calculations phobics find helpful include:

* A form for charting the ups and downs of a panic attack and the levels of anxiety in general is given in the Appendix.

· Determining how much a total purchase will cost.
· Estimating the number of people in a room or a theater.
· Balancing checkbooks; budgeting; figuring the evening's expenses or the mileage driven on a particular trip.
· Adding the ages of a family or of some other group of people; adding their weights; determining their average height.
· Calculating how many words there are in a particular book; how many days to the next holiday; how much debt there is remaining on the mortgage; and so on.
· Timing events such as traffic lights; elevator rides; sermons in church; the trip across a bridge, through a tunnel, or from one highway exit to the next. The principal purpose this serves—as is true for all these tools—is to distract the phobic from his sense of losing control. Another important benefit, though, is to demonstrate just how short-lived most phobic situations are. Crossing most bridges takes only a minute or two, at most four or five. A long red light lasts about a minute, an elevator ride only seconds. As indicated earlier, timing the panic attack itself is helpful for the same reasons. Usually it lasts at its worst only a very few minutes.

iv. Physical activities that demand attention. Certain complicated activities are so well rehearsed they become automatic and are no distraction from whatever the individual is thinking. These include most of what occupies people during the course of a day: walking, washing, dressing, combing one's hair, cooking, driving an automobile, knitting, ironing clothes, bathing the children, shopping, scrubbing the floor, and so on. Many business assignments also have this routine character. Sports such as swimming, jogging, or bicycling also can be mindless in this sense, which is why doing push-ups or running around the block does not make one less anxious.* On the other hand, sports that are not so accustomed can occupy all of one's attention—first learning how to swim, for example, or first learning how to bicycle. Activities that are familiar can be made unfamiliar by doing them somewhat differently. Competitive sports work best of all. Everyone can find some activity that is interesting to engage in, whether it is reading a particular book, painting, cooking something special, or making love. As these few examples suggest, pleasurable activities work best. Even the modest endeavor of doodling, however, can serve to make an otherwise intolerable situation much less so.

v. Games. Among the games phobics find helpful are Auto-bridge, crossword puzzles, video games, word games, table games, and made-up games such as playing "poker" with the license plates of passing cars. Card games that involve others are inherently more interesting but may be threatening if the phobic feels trapped in that setting. In any case, he needs to develop tools he can use even when he is alone. The variety of games a creative person such as the typical phobic can invent is prodigious. Figuring out the time of sunset is one; betting on the number of steps in a stairway is another.

vi. Fantasy. Phobics have extraordinary imaginations. If they could not see so clearly the imaginary dangers of becoming panicky, they would not withdraw and so would not become phobic in the first place. Their ability to fantasize was used as the basis

---

* These were the first things I tried when I became phobic. Feeling panicky I felt full of nervous energy, as if I *should* be running somewhere.

for an early treatment of agoraphobia. Some people could get levels of anxiety in the calm of a therapist's office simply by closing their eyes and *picturing* themselves in a phobic situation. They could then learn to turn off these anxious feelings by practicing relaxation exercises or by picturing more pleasant scenes such as lying placidly under a tree on a warm spring day. It was possible for some patients to desensitize themselves in such a way, although the real phobic situation tends to have more impact than one strictly imagined. Even in that real situation, however, the use of imagery can serve to distract. With practice the phobic can turn his attention from his circumstances to some imagined situation that is more pleasant. Fantasies that are dramatic or exhilarating have the best chance of occupying the phobic's attention. Some people dwell on past victories, athletic or business, or future successes. Some take part in an imaginary argument. A few otherwise well-behaved middle-aged ladies mutter imprecations under their breath as they wait for an elevator. It is quite possible for some people to tolerate the discomfort of a classroom or a drive across town by imagining sexual encounters with people sitting nearby or glimpsed along the way.* As is true with the use of all the tools, training is required for success. Empty daydreaming is too passive to work.

Phobics reading these pages will surely find it difficult to believe that any of these techniques will work for them. The anxiety they experience seems overwhelming and quite beyond such simple tricks of the mind. At first glance what is suggested seems no more than advice to "relax" or

---

* It is hard to recommend to phobics, who are circumspect and prim for the most part, that they engage in sexual daydreams, especially when they are preoccupied at those times with thoughts of dying or going crazy! I do so for the same reason I mention these other tools: They work for some people. These are mostly men. Or perhaps men are more willing to admit to sexual fantasies.

"hang on" or "think about something positive for a change." It is an understandable reaction. The actual process by which someone—anyone—learns to control his thoughts and behavior *in whatever context* is so subtle it is difficult to convey through the written word. Not very different would be trying to teach someone to swim by means of a written manual alone—especially if that person did not believe it was possible for human beings to swim. Yet if the directions were clear enough and if that person were willing to go into the water long enough to give them a try, he might very well learn how to swim. If he did, he would likely have trouble explaining to another nonswimmer just how he had managed it. "I put my arms out there one after another then slapped my feet against the surface of the water, and after a while I didn't sink anymore!" That would not sound convincing to someone who knows from past experience that whenever *he* goes into a pool he immediately sinks to the bottom. "It might be possible for others to swim," he would say dubiously if he had not actually seen other people swimming, but he himself is simply "too heavy."

In order to make more vivid this process by which the phobic learns to master his anxiety, I give these three detailed accounts. At best they are a motion picture of people who are "too heavy" to swim but who are swimming nevertheless simply by "moving one arm after the other." In the end, though, it is not possible to learn how to swim without getting wet. The phobic learns how to cope with the phobic situation only by going into it. He learns how to manage his anxious feelings only by becoming anxious.

Although Theresa felt uncomfortable in many different places —tall buildings and open-air garages, for example—she spent much of the time when she began practicing trying to get used to a small bookstore not very far from her home. In the systematic way in which she usually did things, she marked down on various lists all the actions that in the past had seemed to distract her from the fears that otherwise preoccupied her. They amounted to a rough list of tools, including both tools of rote and tools of concentration. In order to cope with the discomfort she experienced simply standing at the threshold of the store, she first tried singing to herself. It was a song she was familiar with from childhood and which she associated with pleasant times. It did not help. Neither did saying the alphabet backwards, tapping her shoe on the ground in a complicated rhythm, or trying to remember all the states that begin with the letter A. Throughout she remained just as uncomfortable as she usually did confronting a phobic situation—although not quite as awful as she had expected. Referring to a list she had made up ahead of time, she tried these various things one after the other:

1. Counting the customers
2. Playing with a rubber band encircling her wrist
3. Eating candy (three candy bars altogether)
4. Keeping track of the remaining few minutes before her helper picked her up

During this period of time she was anxious to varying degrees —one brief moment feeling relatively comfortable, the next as if she could not tolerate remaining another minute. Later on she thought in retrospect that she might perhaps have been a little calmer by the time she started eating the candy. Although it did not seem to her these tools had helped her especially, she did admit that as a matter of fact she was able to wait longer in that stressful setting than she would have thought possible. During the next few days she returned to the bookstore over and over again, remaining inside at least fifteen minutes and once a half hour. She tried to distract herself from her circumstance by:

1. Keeping track of how many customers came into the store only to browse and how many purchased books
2. Sucking hard candy
3. Pinching herself
4. Praying
5. Making sketches of the building across the way
6. Talking to a friend who happened to come by
7. Figuring out what to cook for dinner
8. Adding up the money she had in her wallet
9. Keeping track of the passersby

Of these activities, talking to her friend was most interesting and consequently worked best to lower her level of anxiety. Unfortunately, as she pointed out, friends cannot be relied on to walk by at just the right moment. But drawing also calmed her somewhat, she thought; not entirely and not every time, but to a noticeable extent.

"Maybe because I'm a professional artist," she said. "I can't draw well while I'm standing up, so I get annoyed with myself. In the meantime, I forget about being nervous."

Another tool she found helpful was trying to match each customer with the kind of book he was buying—a tool of concentration. She found looking at the books themselves diverting, particularly art books and puzzle books. Not helpful were attempts to add up the prices of a number of books or timing other people's activities—also tools of concentration. She could not keep her attention fixed on these complicated and not very interesting tasks, nor were most of the tools of rote helpful, such as:

1. Playing with car keys
2. Counting backwards from a hundred, three at a time
3. Pinching herself
4. Feeling the texture of the book covers
5. Chewing gum
6. Walking up and down the aisles
7. Reading the titles of the books

During the following days and weeks, as Theresa came slowly to overcome her fear of bookstores, libraries, and ultimately every other place, she developed lists of tools appropriate to those places and activities. Drawing and talking to people worked best. When she went driving, she could not draw, of course, so she talked about her feelings into a tape recorder, used a CB radio, or sang out loud. On the other hand, when trying to cope with her fears of heights by climbing to the top of an open-air garage, she took along a drawing pad and pencils. At first when she became panicky she stopped walking and began to draw anything, even stick figures. Toward the end of treatment simply holding a pencil would bring a panic attack quickly to an end! It was as if the pencil had come to symbolize her ability to control her anxious feelings or, perhaps, her certain knowledge by that time that her feelings could not hurt no matter how extreme.

Of all the other tools she tried, only one seemed to work at all: Fiddling with a child's whistle that she carried about with her brought her "back to reality" and lessened her distress.

When Perry began to practice confronting phobic situations, it seemed that none of the tools he tried would work. When he stepped across the threshold of an elevator, the idea of counting things or timing things or feeling things seemed preposterous. Talking to a helper who accompanied him did make him less anxious, but he thought it was because the mere presence of a familiar person made him feel more secure rather than because of any interaction between them. When he agreed at the urging of the helper to try actually using tools, he found he was unable to keep them in mind when the elevator lurched into motion. Instead, he clenched his fists and tried to control his breathing as he always did, neither of which helped at all. Making up a list ahead of time didn't seem to help either, since he was inclined to misplace the list, and by the time he found it the elevator ride was over. Or, by mistake, he took out a laundry list or the list of tools he had drawn up for practicing in a car. He could scarcely play "license-plate poker" in an elevator. When he did finally get around to trying the tools he had planned—making detailed notes of his feelings or timing the elevator ride or chewing candy —none seemed to alleviate his anxious feelings, although he did report grudgingly that the ride seemed not to take quite as long as usual. If that was so, however, he attributed it to his frustration over being asked to attempt these petty maneuvers when he felt he was barely able to stand up! But he was less skeptical only a week later. Maybe he was just getting used to elevators, he said, but he began to notice a general lessening of his fear. The possibility of getting trapped in the elevator seemed less likely and less threatening, and perhaps it was true that chewing on a hard candy distracted him, momentarily at least, from the fact of his riding in the elevator. Maybe. Certainly he recognized by then that talking to a helper (even more than listening to him) made him less anxious. More difficult for Perry was confronting his primary phobia—driving. Chewing candy, helpful though it may have been in an elevator, did not work while he was driving an automobile. It was not enough of a distraction. Indeed, he found it hard to concentrate on any tools. Once again he lost the list of tools he carried with him to jog his memory. Talking to the phobia aide sitting next to him helped somewhat, but listening to the radio, smoking cigarettes, and counting the bumps on the steering wheel did not; and taking written notes while driving was impossible. Still, in only a week or so he *was* driving, and it was plain to him then, however skeptical he may have been at first, that certain tools *were* working reliably to make him less anxious. Of these the most important were:

1. Talking—to anyone: passengers, pedestrians from whom he asked directions, or even himself
2. Keeping track of the ups and downs of his level of anxiety by timing them and making report of them into a tape recorder
3. Chewing hard candy (and later on other kinds of food). Eating, surprisingly, suppressed the thought of vomiting that had troubled him for years whenever he felt panicky.

At first these tools were helpful when he was only slightly anxious, but after some time they worked, although to a lesser extent, when his distress was extreme. Once when he was stuck in a traffic jam, seemingly forever, he became unequivocally panicky every few minutes but found he could stop the feeling each time by talking to other drivers through the car window. With more practice other tools began to work as well, including a few that had previously seemed useless or impossible, such as writing detailed notes. And those tools that defeated the panic attacks in one situation worked equally well in others, even when there had been no opportunity to practice! For example, when Perry flew in an airplane for the first time, he felt just as panicky as if he were in an elevator or an automobile, but when he began to take notes those feelings diminished abruptly, leaving him "strangely calm." As time went on, writing a few words on a note pad was enough to abort the attack! By then the whole phobia struck him as "a waste of time." He had come to think of the panic attack as insignificant, "like hitting my elbow on the funny bone. It hurts like hell for a minute, but it doesn't mean anything." And he no longer bothered with tools. It was as if he sneered inwardly at the panicky feelings on those rare occasions when they returned, and that was enough to dispel them.

Janet attributed her recovery from agoraphobia to a few tools that seemed to her "almost magical" in their effect. Like Theresa and Perry, she tried a number of tools of rote and concentration during the first few days of enthusiastic practice—without much success. She persisted nevertheless, demonstrating the stubbornness, determination, and willingness to go beyond what is required that makes obvious who will eventually get well. One day when she was standing just inside the entrance to a beauty parlor, frantically trying one thing after another to lessen the anxiety she always felt in that place, her attention was drawn to a magazine lying open on a nearby table. There was an article in view about someone she knew, a friend from childhood who had become an actress. She began reading the story and looked up a few minutes later to realize that she was feeling fine! All of her distress had been dispelled by the act of reading. She could not even remember the moment it had gone. From then on she carried movie magazines everywhere, and if she entered into a phobic situation, reading them usually helped.

On a different occasion she was sitting at home alone reading a book about heart disease, as she had been instructed to do by her therapist. Her long-standing concern about having a heart attack was often made worse temporarily by hearing about or reading about someone else's heart condition. That was the result, he told her, of knowing not enough rather than too much. But she became anxious again as usual. She felt better briefly after talking to her husband on the telephone and then to her therapist, but then found herself once again pacing desperately around her living room. She tried reading but could not concentrate. She was too nervous to eat. Cooking was no distraction. Hurriedly she tried counting objects, taking notes, playing cards, and looking out the window, all without noticeable effect. Finally she sat down angrily to write a complaining letter to her therapist who had misled her into thinking that these tools would work.

When she was halfway through the letter she realized she was no longer afraid. Getting angry—and the act of writing—had substituted for being afraid. From then on she found she could reliably lower her level of anxiety by getting angry. When she had to wait on line at restaurants, she complained to the head waiter—behavior somewhat out of character for her—and felt better. She muttered under her breath in beauty parlors. And writing itself became an effective tool. When she had to wait in a dentist's office or even in church, she wrote letters or took notes for writing letters. If she was only a little anxious to begin with, she became calm, but even if she was panicky, those feelings also diminished to manageable proportions. *And what worked to control her anxiety in one setting worked equally well in others.* As often happens in exposure therapy, Janet was troubled along the way with *new* symptoms of anxiety; in her case a sense of choking came upon her for no discernible reason once when she was shopping, but that feeling yielded in turn promptly to these tools.

Certain aspects of these cases should be underlined because they are so common:

1. Progress is slow and inconsistent. To expect more, especially at the beginning of treatment, is to be disappointed. Over time, real progress, obvious even to a skeptical person, takes place. Rarely does anyone begin treatment with high hopes. Blind faith is not necessary, but a willingness to follow directions is. Confidence in the effectiveness of treatment comes only after the first few successes. It comes then sometimes with the force of revelation: "Holy smoke, it really works!"

2. Although the panic attack is likely to be experienced the same way throughout treatment—in fact, usually throughout the course of the illness—the other symptoms of anxiety change. Someone troubled by a choking feeling may find it diminishing during treatment only to be replaced by another that is equally disconcerting: shortness of breath, dizziness, or palpitations. Most typical of all is a feeling of unreality, which can be especially upsetting and

frightening. This feeling of strangeness probably represents nothing more than the sense of *unfamiliarity* that strikes as people begin entering into situations and circumstances they had been avoiding sometimes for years. As these various new feelings become less threatening, they too disappear.

3. Coping successfully with panic attacks in one setting allows the phobic to cope reliably with attacks in other settings even when he has not had the opportunity to practice in these other places. In other words, the phobic who knows how to blunt the force of a panic attack need not be afraid of it no matter where he is and no matter what he is doing.

4. The tools that serve in the beginning to lower the level of anxiety only a little can later on, with practice, bring the most extreme panic attack quickly to an end. Consequently, there comes a time when the patient is no longer truly afraid of the panic attack, no matter how awful it feels. At this point it is unlikely the phobic will withdraw from any situation simply because he becomes panicky. It is at this point also that he may begin to repeat phrases to himself that seem to have a magical calming effect:

"I just tell myself, 'Float through it,' and before I know it the feeling is gone."

"I have this little prayer I say putting me in God's hands. His will be done, so why should I worry?"

"I repeat, 'I'm relaxing my fingers, my arms, my shoulders,' and in a minute or two I'm all relaxed."

"I tell myself, 'What the hell; if you're going to die, you're going to die. I'm tired of living this way.' "

These formulas are not enough at the beginning of treatment to make the phobic less anxious. They are reassuring later on not because of their content but because they are symbolic statements of the phobic's growing conviction that there really is nothing to fear. He can say to himself, "So what if I die?" only because he has come to know that he will not die.

5. The usually futile struggle of phobics to determine the cause of their panic attacks may bring some results toward the end of treatment. At this point, when attacks occur only infrequently, the circumstances may give some indication of those unconscious feelings or impulses that are threatening to break through to the surface.

6. Most phobics put aside these tools at the very end of treatment. If they should get panicky, which may still happen now and then for a while, they are more likely simply to turn their attention back to whatever they were doing the moment before. The panic attack is not much of a distraction. Sometimes they feel surprised or taken aback for a moment. Sometimes they even laugh.

In summary, what you must learn as a phobic is that your anxiety, although an involuntary, automatic response, is first of all not dangerous and second of all subject to your control. Waiting passively allows the feeling to rise unbearably until there seems no alternative to running away, but an active stance works against this process. These tools—the tools of rote and the tools of concentration—are devices to help you become active in thought and behavior. With persistent use they become an alternative to the phobic defense of withdrawal. Coping with the panic attack for only a few minutes at a time makes clear eventually that it is self-limited, without effect except to frighten and enervate. Whenever a real danger presents itself, the panic vanishes immediately as the individual is forced to turn to a real problem and do whatever needs to be done. The mechanism by which panic is dissipated in a graduated exposure therapy is the same: a transformation into activity. What the panic attack represents, remember, is the "fight or flight" reaction. A phobia develops because a particular awful feeling is associated with a particular place or set of circumstances. The phobic becomes panicky and almost as a reflex withdraws. What is recommended in these pages is a strategy for fighting rather than running away. It is not an easy thing to learn. Practice, considerable practice, is required. Therefore, the cardinal rule of this stage of treatment, as it was of the previous stage, is *go a few feet farther, stay a few moments longer*—even when you are very anxious, even panicky. In less time than you think, you will outlast the panic attack, and the fear of it will no longer rule your life.

FEELINGS TO COPE WITH AT THIS STAGE: generalized anxiety and panic.

Chapter 6

STAGE SIX: GETTING PAST "STUCK POINTS"

No matter how successful the exposure therapy, each patient comes to places where it seems he cannot go no matter how hard he tries or finds himself in circumstances that seem intolerable no matter what he does. These are called "stuck points." They are usually manifested concretely at a physical threshold: the inability to cross a particular intersection or bridge, or to venture past a certain floor in a building. Sometimes the threshold is in time, as in the inability to remain home alone overnight. It is unclear why these particular obstacles loom so large, especially to someone who has already mastered one phobic situation after another. It may be that these new places are threatening because they stimulate special feelings such as anger—at the prospect of being left alone, for example. Or they may be difficult because they have taken on a special meaning. A particular floor in a department store may be remembered as a place where an especially awful panic attack or series of panic attacks occurred. A particular intersection at the edge of the patient's perimeter may come to symbolize the frightening aspect of the world outside or a final break with those who helped him and took care of him throughout his illness. Subjectively, the phobic feels only that this particular step, whatever it may be, is simply too long, more like crossing a crevasse than a threshold. In any case, it is the next step and must be taken for therapy to proceed. The task of this stage of treatment is to get past these stuck points quickly, before the hope of recovery dims.

INSTRUCTIONS

Break down the task into smaller, doable pieces. *Every* step can in principle be divided into smaller, more manageable steps. It is this principle that underlies every aspect of an exposure therapy. The problem represented by a stuck point, however, is precisely that in that particular situation it does not seem possible to divide the task. Consider the examples just mentioned. This is how they were described by the affected persons:

"Every day I drive up one block away from this big intersection and stop. I just can't go right on through. It's got a red light that takes five minutes. You can't make a U-turn, and the traffic piles up in every direction. If I got there and something happened, I'd be stuck."

"I can stay by myself now the whole afternoon. That's because I know if I call my husband, he can run right over from his job. Besides, there's a neighbor next door. And I keep myself busy cooking. But if I'm all by myself the whole night, there isn't anything I can do or anybody I can call. Not in the middle of the night. My husband should be taking business trips, but I won't let him. Suppose something happened? The night lasts forever."

"I do okay in this department store up until the third floor. The first two floors took me a couple of weeks to get used to. I went up one step at a time. The last step took me two whole days, coming back to it over and over, but the only way up to the third floor is an escalator. That's like one giant step. Suppose I have to get off right in the middle?"

In all three of these cases, a week or more of daily practice was required before the stuck point was passed. Often, months go by before that place becomes truly comfortable. Although the length of time required to get past these obstacles varies, depending more on the amount of time spent practicing than on any difficulty inherent in those special circumstances, the process in each case is remarkably similar. Given below in brief outline are the steps by which each patient succeeded. Left out are the details of their emotional reactions. Most of the time, as usual, they were uncomfortable although rarely panicky. There were also moments of exhilaration, even triumph.

Getting Past an Unpassable Intersection

Step 1: Approach the intersection on foot with a helper.

Step 2: Loiter about the intersection. Keep track of the flow of traffic. Time the light.

Step 3: Return again and again, still on foot, but at a different time of day. Return finally alone.

Step 4: Imagine yourself at the wheel of one of the cars stopped at the intersection. *Try* to get anxious this way. Then, using the tools described previously, try to lower the level of the anxiety. The tools should be appropriate for use in a car; for example, speaking into a tape recorder or keeping track of out-of-state license plates. This exercise should be repeated until boredom sets in.

Step 5: Drive with a helper into the intersection from the least threatening direction and at the time of day when there is the least traffic.

Step 6: Drive with a helper, or ride as a passenger if that is less frightening, into the intersection from the hardest direction, but in the lane closest to the curb. Being close to the curb makes it possible to stop the car and get out, if that seems necessary. *

Step 7: Drive through the intersection with a helper sitting next to you in the front passenger seat; the next time in the back seat visible to you in the rearview mirror; then out of sight directly behind you.

Step 8: Finally, go through the intersection all alone— over and over again.

Should one of these steps itself become a stuck point, there are still smaller steps possible. For example, a helper can be standing at the intersection while the phobic drives by. Or the phobic may find he is able to make a right turn at the intersection when he cannot yet drive directly across it. Sometimes tranquilizers used only once or twice make it possible to take a step that otherwise seems too difficult.

Confronting the Night that "Lasts Forever"

Step 1: Spend a lot of time home alone during the day, slowly extending the tolerable hours of the afternoon into the evening and then into the night. Meaningful progress from one day to the next may be measured in minutes.

Step 2: A reliable person should stand by at the other end of the telephone. Whether or not you are particularly anxious at these practice sessions, make a point of calling him. Believing he is within reach and *knowing* it are two different things. As in many other aspects of exposure therapy, you must learn the truth by finding out for yourself. The reliable person should understand that if you feel unable to tolerate being by yourself any longer, he has to return home. You should know ahead of time how long that trip will take.

Step 3: Keep close at hand the tools that have helped you so far. Cooking and other household occupations may not be enough since the fear of being at home alone developed in the context of doing these things. This suggests

---

* Almost certainly it will not.

that they are not by themselves sufficient distraction from the panicky feelings.

Step 4: Have in mind some place to go should the anxiety seem intolerable. Do not hesitate to visit a neighbor, even late at night, or some public establishment such as a restaurant that might be open.

Step 5: Try to insure that sleep comes readily the first night of being alone. Exercise beforehand so that you are tired. If necessary, take a sleeping pill. That night a spouse or other close family member should sleep within traveling distance at a relative's home or at a nearby motel.

Step 6: Remain alone the next few nights, if necessary still with the help of medication. The trusted person can be further away, finally away altogether on a business trip. Even then he should be available by telephone, and so should other friends and family.

Taking a Giant Step One Small Step at a Time: Escalators

Step 1: Spend a lot of time looking at the escalator, in particular watching the people as they ascend. Their calm is contagious.

Step 2: Time their ascent. How long does it take for someone who is walking or running up the moving stairway? Five seconds? Ten seconds?

Step 3: Imagine yourself on the escalator. Watch the floor below recede, the floor above come closer. *Try* to feel anxious, then try not to. Continue until you are no longer able to feel anxious no matter how hard you try.

Step 4: Feel the moving banister. If possible, get quickly on the escalator and off again. If that seems too difficult to do in a crowded store, getting very close and observing people stepping on will be enough.

Step 5: While standing near the escalator, practice lowering your level of anxiety by using the tools that have made it possible for you to cope previously with stairs or other phobic circumstances. Talking to someone, making detailed notes, keeping track of other people, unwrapping candies are all appropriate to this brief but threatening trial. *

Step 6: With a helper standing either directly in front of you or directly behind, get on the escalator. This first ride should be made as comfortable as possible. If you feel better holding onto the railing with both hands, that is what you should do. If you feel better standing in the exact middle of the step, that is what you should do. If you feel better sitting down on the escalator, that is what you should do! †

Step 7: Take the escalator by yourself but with your helper waiting on the floor below or the floor above you. Use tools whether or not you feel anxious.

Step 8: Ride the escalator by yourself over and over again until all fear is gone and boredom sets in.

From these examples it can be seen that every stuck point can be attacked systematically in the same way:

Examine the stuck point from every point of view— literally by going to the place and looking at it and figuratively by considering every possible consequence of entering into the situation. The reality, whatever it may be, is always less frightening than what you can imagine. Dwell on that reality. *Spend time* in or near that place. If other people are present, you will be reassured by their lack of concern. Calm is communicable and contagious.

Get as close to the stuck point as you can, then closer. If it is a particular place, go foot by foot, if necessary inch by inch. Come at it from a different direction so that it seems to you just a little different. If the stuck point is

---

* A stuck point may consist of a task that takes only a few moments from beginning to end, but may hold up progress indefinitely nevertheless.

† This is very unlikely, given the phobic's penchant for remaining inconspicuous.

located in time instead of space—for example, remaining home alone overnight or staying in a church or classroom for the allotted time—enter into it first for just a moment, if necessary just the briefest moment. *It is permissible to enter a classroom or a church for just a moment and then leave.* * It is the unwillingness of some phobics to take such an in-between step, which seems embarrassing to them and of little significance, that allows stuck points to develop. Getting up and leaving does *not* create a disturbance, let alone a spectacle, and is readily understood by anyone to whom the reason is explained.

Plan these retreats. Figure out a way of exiting gracefully from the stuck point. There may be different exits depending on how far you have progressed into that situation. For example, getting off a bank line is easier when you are in the middle of the line than when you are in front making a transaction. In one situation you can simply say "excuse me" and leave. In the other you may have to ask the teller to hold your money! Very likely you will not need to escape, but it is reassuring to know that you can.

Use a helper! All those things a helper provides are most useful at stuck points: suggestions, distraction, comfort and, perhaps most important of all, company. What can be done first only with a helper should be tried later on with the helper at a distance. Going through the stuck point all by yourself should be postponed until the very end.

Use tools! The tools that have proven helpful in practicing up to the point of getting stuck should be tried first. It may be possible also to devise something especially appropriate to the stuck point. Someone having trouble making purchases at a store counter, for instance, may choose to buy something the first time at a cheese store or a candy shop where it is permissible to sample the wares while

---

* Or a theater, or a restaurant, or a dinner party, or a ball game, or a business meeting, or a beauty parlor, or a bus ride.

waiting. If one tool doesn't seem to help, try another. Persistence is what counts.

Go into and past the stuck point *in very small steps.* Just as a line can be divided geometrically into ever smaller segments, so can a stuck point. Progress can be measured in tiny increments. Struggling stubbornly to make this slow, almost imperceptible advance is finally rewarded when, sometimes without warning, one finds it possible to go the rest of the way all at once. The process is akin to pounding on a boulder with a sledgehammer, chipping away one small piece after another until abruptly the rock shatters.

Each of these small in-between steps should be repeated over and over again. Then, when you have finally succeeded in getting past the stuck point, do that again and again. However terrified you may have been at first, you will feel simply weary and bored in the end. Finally, no longer able to dwell on the experience itself, you will begin to think about other things—those personal matters that preoccupy everyone when they walk about, drive somewhere, or engage in other such accustomed, largely automatic activities.

These steps for getting past a stuck point can be seen to resemble the larger steps by which the phobia itself is defeated. The affected person, in the company of a helper and using tools to distract himself, enters systematically into the frightening situation a little at a time until the fear is seen to be unrealistic. Success depends on practice and persistence.

Other common examples of stuck points and the steps by which they were defeated are given below:

Getting Out of the House

A woman was so agoraphobic she had not left her apartment for the previous twenty years; indeed, for the last few years she felt uncomfortable everywhere except her own bedroom. With the help of a therapist who visited her in her home, she was able after a few sessions to go out of her bedroom and her apartment into the street but found she could go no further no matter how hard she tried.

1. She confronted this stuck point first with her therapist present. She stood with him for a half hour at a time just outside the entrance to her apartment building.
2. When there was little pedestrian traffic, she walked back and forth repeatedly from where he stood at the doorway to the curb about ten feet away.
3. She practiced this small walk repeatedly at various times of the day and with various people standing by.
4. With the therapist standing in the middle of the sidewalk, she walked a little way down the street, counting off the seconds and the steps.
5. With the therapist present but out of sight, she walked unsteadily to the end of the block—counting her steps, losing count, and beginning to count again.
6. With no one in sight, she walked all the way around the block—still counting her steps. She went without hesitation past a shortcut she had planned to take should her level of anxiety have risen unbearably.
7. *Only a week later* she was walking by herself everywhere!

Animal Phobias

A young woman fearful all her life of small animals had become within the last year so phobic of dogs in particular that she was unable to leave her home. During three months of treatment she had improved sufficiently to walk through the streets in sight of a dog if the dog was properly leashed, but she could not bring herself to pet the dog.

1. A particularly compliant, somnolent, very old dog was borrowed from a friend and put safely inside a playpen. From the other end of the room the woman studied the dog.

2. At a distance she walked about the playpen, slowly approaching then backing away again, as the dog, otherwise inert, turned his head slowly to look at her.
3. With a friend standing nearby, she leaned over and petted the animal over a period of twenty minutes until she felt entirely at ease.
4. Then, with the dog outside the playpen, she continued to pet him.*
5. She went through these small steps again with a puppy. If the first dog seemed moribund, this one was bouncy and full of life, unpredictable, but certainly not threatening to any ordinary person. Still, it was an hour before she could pick up the dog.
6. Finally, she held the puppy in her lap, long enough for both of them to calm down.

A woman with a pigeon phobia approached pigeons closer and closer over a period of months, pretending that she was a creature much larger and scarier than a pigeon, as indeed she was. Each time, when she could come no closer, she jumped at them, frightening them away before they could fly en masse at her. Of course they flew in the other direction. This simple device led her past the point where she had felt stuck—about five feet away from the birds.

A woman afraid of snakes progressed similarly over a period of eight weeks from an inability to go into any grassy area because of her fear of snakes—a fear so profound she was unable even to look at photographs of snakes —to a ready willingness to hold large snakes in her hands! Along the way she engaged in these exercises:

1. Looking at drawings of snakes, then at photographs
2. Holding a cloth toy sewn into the shape of a snake
3 Holding a real snake skin and leaving the skin on a hall table until it became familiar

---

* Typically, she played down this success. "The dog was so placid, I thought he was dead."

4. Going with a helper to a pet store where she could watch a live snake through the walls of a glass aquarium
5. Tapping on the walls of the aquarium. (The typical snake is more lethargic and difficult to rouse than the sleepiest dog)
6. Watching with a helper from the safety of a doorway while a herpetologist wound a snake around his arm
7. Touching the snake briefly
8. Holding the snake

Both these women made a similar discovery: most small animals, rather than leaping out at a human being, will go as fast as possible in the other direction. Pigeons fly away. Snakes slither away. Even poisonous snakes will escape given a chance.

A Tunnel Phobia

A man afraid of riding in any public conveyance had managed, with the help of a phobia aide, to venture a few stops on a train but was stuck at that point because he would have to travel through a long tunnel in order to arrive at the next station. It did not seem to him he could tolerate such a prolonged ride without losing control of himself and becoming hysterical.

1. He found out from others exactly how long the trip would take, at what point the train went around a curve, when it traveled slowly, when it speeded up, how much noise other passing trains made, whether there were exits in the tunnel should he have to leave the train because of a fire, and so on.
2. He planned the trip with his aide: whether to sit or stand throughout the trip or walk from car to car, whether or not to talk to someone and if so to whom, and which tools to bring along.
3. After taking a tranquilizer, and accompanied by his aide, he finally boarded the train and went through the tunnel. He took notes and timed different aspects of the

trip, but most of the time he talked animatedly to his aide about his plans for the future.

4. That same day he went back and forth two more times without the aide, occupying himself with a difficult crossword puzzle.

5. The following week he went by himself to meet a friend and was so involved in a conversation with the person sitting next to him that he did not realize he had gone all the way through the tunnel until after the train came out the other side.

Driving

A middle-aged woman who had been afraid of traveling had progressed with treatment to the point where she could be a passenger in a car if her husband drove, but she could not drive herself.

1. She sat in the driver's seat of the car with her husband, who was acting as her helper, sitting alongside. They talked about the various difficulties she was likely to encounter driving through the neighborhood.

2. She sat in the car by herself, *imagining* driving from one place to another, confronting one obstacle after another. She planned which tools to use to lower her level of anxiety, and she figured out where she could turn around if she suddenly felt she could go no farther.

3. She set the car into motion, driving back and forth the length of her driveway. When her neighbor asked what she was doing, she explained. She was not deterred by any embarrassment she may have felt.

4. The next day she drove slowly down the block and then around the block, back to where she had started. She repeated this exercise four or five times in a row on three successive days.

5. She drove across town, timing each light she came to and counting and keeping track of various makes of automobiles.

6. A month later she was driving comfortably everywhere in town.

Going to a Restaurant

A woman who felt uneasy among groups of people was able after a month of treatment to tolerate small family gatherings, but she could not go into restaurants. If she ate in front of strangers, she thought she might become so anxious she would choke. Merely walking into the restaurant seemed impossible.

1. The woman's son found a nearby family restaurant that was so small it had only a few tables. The proprietor was a friendly person familiar to everyone in the neighborhood. The phobic woman found, however, that she could not enter into even this relatively unthreatening place. So she began by sitting in a car parked outside the restaurant, watching while patrons entered and left. She ate part of a sandwich from time to time. She tried to imagine she was eating the sandwich inside the restaurant.

2. On another occasion she stood for a long while directly outside the restaurant.

3. The next day, when the restaurant was first open and still empty to customers, she hovered at the entranceway, literally one foot in and one foot out.

4. Only a few minutes later she was able to sit briefly at a table opposite her son. She rose abruptly and left, only to return again a moment later.

5. While her son ate, she sat down part of the time and the rest of the time went to the bathroom or talked to her husband on the telephone or conversed with the owner of the restaurant. Once she left to buy cigarettes at a corner store.

6. The following day she was able to sit relatively comfortably in the restaurant watching others who had come to eat dinner.

7. The next day she sat by herself at a corner table, nibbling at some food intermittently, bouncing up and down to make telephone calls, and the rest of the time reading with difficulty a spy novel she had brought along. By the end of the evening, she said she was "relaxed."

8. Later that week she ate dinner at a more formal restaurant, still sitting at an out-of-the-way table, though, and getting up every few minutes.

9. It was not until a full year later that she could eat anywhere she chose, but by then dining out had become "one of the great pleasures" of her life.

Heights

A young man inducted into the army was so afraid of heights that he could not go above the third floor where, as it happened, his detachment was assigned to sleep. His commanding officer informed him and the psychiatrist posted to the base that he expected this emotional problem to be cleared up "at once—or else." Even with this additional motivation to get well, the soldier found himself stuck at the very beginning of treatment in the stairwell leading to the third floor.

1. He sat with the psychiatrist on the first step talking about all the things he could imagine going wrong, which included falling out of a window.

2. After ten minutes they moved up to the next step. Sitting at this barely increased elevation proved too painful, however, and immediately the soldier slipped down to the first step.

3. Because of the pressure of time, the psychiatrist thought it best to sedate the soldier before trying again. He prescribed enough medicine to put most people promptly to sleep. The soldier remained awake, however, and fearful, although plainly very sleepy. Nevertheless, in this partly clouded state of mind he became

more compliant and could be led up to the third floor in one fell swoop.

4. He sat in a chair near a window, the psychiatrist sitting next to him. After a while the soldier fell asleep.
5. When he awoke he looked out the window until the sense of vertigo and the thought of falling or jumping out had passed.
6. He leaned against the window, testing its strength and his resolve.
7. The next day, without medication but with the psychiatrist still next to him, he walked up another flight to the roof of the building. He went up the last few steps on his hands and knees.
8. He walked about on the roof, feeling occasional urges to run to the edge and throw himself off. He discovered by timing them that these particularly awful feelings lasted only three or four seconds.
9. He stayed on the roof *all day*, toward the end all by himself, until he could feel comfortable leaning over the edge.

This whole process from beginning to end took two days.

Sitting Up Front in Church

A very religious woman had been unable to attend church for many years because she thought she might lose control of herself in that quiet, sanctified setting and embarrass herself by fainting, crying out, or in some other way creating a fuss. With therapy she had managed to get into the church, and within the space of a month even further to an aisle seat at the rear of the church, but not past that point.

1. She sat at her usual place on the aisle carrying her usual tools: a Bible and a watch to time the various portions of the service. On this occasion, though, her helper sat next to her, where she could grab hold of him if she

became too anxious. After a time they changed seats so that she was no longer sitting on the aisle.

2. That evening they went back to the church. This time she sat two seats from the aisle and her helper sat in front of her. As they planned, she left for a moment at a convenient point, then returned.

3. The following evening, at a sparsely attended service, they again sat near each other, but one row closer to the front of the church.

4. They went to services again the following day but at a different church. This time she sat two rows further down and her helper sat across the aisle.

5. Two weeks later she was sitting by herself in church wherever she chose, although still uneasy from time to time and at least on one occasion panicky.

These examples can be multiplied endlessly. Every situation in life, from flying an airplane to simple conversation, can represent an obstacle and a snare to the phobic —and a stuck point. No impasse is so difficult or long-standing, however, that it does not yield to these simple measures.

FEELINGS TO COPE WITH AT THIS STAGE: discouragement and frustration.

STAGE SEVEN: CONSOLIDATING ACHIEVEMENTS

Progress can be measured by how far into threatening situations the phobic can go and how much anxiety he can tolerate—or how long he can tolerate it—before leaving. The decrease in his anxious feelings that every phobic expects from treatment, and has a right to expect, lags behind. For example, a person with a driving phobia will likely have to practice regularly at a distance of ten to twenty miles from home before he begins to feel comfortable driving in his immediate neighborhood. By the time he feels comfortable at that ten-mile radius, he will have spent considerable time taking much longer trips. The woman described in the last section who worked her way painfully to the front of a church was almost all the way to the front before she could feel really at ease standing at the rear. But there does finally come a time when the phobic can function in many areas without suffering terribly. The initial skepticism he may have felt toward treatment is replaced by the grudging recognition that improvement is possible, although purchased only at the price of hard work and considerable discomfort. It seems strange, therefore, that morale can falter again at this stage. The phobic, now able to do much of what he was previously unable to do—and much of the time without any distress at all—may nevertheless seem dispirited and find reasons for not pursuing treatment as determinedly as before. It may be simply that he is fatigued. In some cases he may be discouraged because he does not recognize what is plain to everyone else—that he is indeed much improved. It is as if he has forgotten or somehow discounts how troubled he was not long ago. He may become clinically depressed. Some patients become depressed, paradoxically, precisely because they know they are better. More independent now, they may face the loss of the parent or spouse with whom they may previously have been in constant company. Others may have to face difficult decisions: Should they remain in a bad marriage now that they are no longer tied to their spouse? Or, now able to work, what sort of work should they do? Often at this point a parent or spouse who has previously encouraged treatment feels threatened by the patient's growing independence and begins to pull the other way. Practicing is more difficult since the areas in which the phobic must go to practice are more inconvenient, likely to be farther away—in the next town, perhaps. Practice requires more time, especially since at this stage new activities such as visiting old friends or even working make other demands on the phobic's time. Yet the gains made so far in treatment are not secure and will disappear without continued practice. As long as there is a perimeter outside of which the phobic feels afraid, his condition is unstable. Those limits can shrink down again as they did in the very beginning of his illness. If the phobic were to become physically ill at this point, with a broken leg, perhaps, or a respiratory infection or any other condition that required him to be indoors for two or three weeks, all the phobic circumstances to which he had adjusted with great effort would once again seem strange to him and threatening—at least temporarily. These various issues must be addressed as they come up. The task of this stage of treatment therefore, is simply to persist.

INSTRUCTIONS

1. Refer to the list you made in the beginning of treatment. How much could you not do then that you can readily do now? In particular, can you tolerate the panicky feelings without running away? Can you make those feelings lessen or go away entirely? Do not make little of the progress you have made. It may well be that you have been struggling to accomplish what others can do effortlessly, but it is a real accomplishment nonetheless. Whatever the causes of a panic disorder and the phobias that come as a result, the obstacles they represent are very real. Overcoming them is harder than earning a college degree—in the judgment of a number of people who have done both.

2. At this point very likely the worst is over. Try to keep that in mind. A sustained effort at this stage will bring you within sight of being really well. You may find yourself in a setback from time to time, unable for one reason or another to do this week what was manageable last week, but

at this stage setbacks are temporary. You are closer to finishing than you think. On the other hand, if you stop practicing, for whatever reason, you run the risk, even at this advanced stage, of losing all the hard-won gains you have made. Just as you "locked in" your ability to go to a particular place by going there over and over again, you make certain you can deal with your panicky feelings by dealing with them over and over again. The tools that worked only a little at first work better and better, and as you become more confident in them, there is less and less reason to avoid any place. And the phobia begins to fade.

3. Do not worry about the possibility that your getting well will have a bad effect on your marriage or on other important relationships. If someone cares about you, he will adjust to your becoming more independent. If the relationship is based on a mutual dependence so extreme it cannot survive your getting well, it probably ought not to survive. In fact, experience indicates that people do adjust. As parents accommodate themselves to an adolescent who begins to stay out late, everyone will adjust to your doing the ordinary things that people commonly do, even if they take you away from home for periods of time. As for any changes you yourself may wish to make either in these relationships or in other aspects of your life—such as changing jobs or moving to another area of the country— these decisions should be put off until later. This is good advice for anyone whose life is changing significantly for whatever reason. You may be resentful now of someone upon whom you have depended constantly for years, for needing someone greatly inevitably leads to resentment. Or you may feel guilt-ridden. Once you are free of that dependence you will likely feel differently. Life itself may seem frightening now that all of life is within reach, but this feeling is not likely to last. When at last you feel confident of recovery, when your illness no longer influences what you do day by day, then you can sensibly decide how you want to spend your life and with whom.

4. Expect to improve at a faster pace. You may not be aware consciously of any changes in the way you think about your illness, but at this stage of treatment you have come largely to accept the two important facts that exposure therapy attempts to teach:

    a. There is nothing truly to fear in the phobic situation. You will not in those circumstances become trapped, get lost, or find yourself desperately alone. You are just as safe in one place as another.

    b. The panic attack itself is not dangerous to you. You will not lose control of yourself. You will not suffer a physical or nervous breakdown.

A third truth is slowly becoming apparent. To a growing extent you can control and diminish your anxious feelings using the tools with which you have been practicing. Your own experience has been your instructor.

Sarah's phobia seemed discrete at first glance, simply a fear of animals rather than the more serious agoraphobia, of which claustrophobia and acrophobia (a fear of heights), for example, are just different forms. But her phobia was of such proportions that she was unable to leave her home for fear of encountering a dog or cat. Her thought that she would *lose control* of herself if she encountered one of these pets and *embarrass* herself by her behavior suggested an underlying agoraphobia. In any case, the treatment for discrete phobias and agoraphobia is the same: a slow, measured introduction into the phobic situation and to the feelings that situation brings on. The use of tools to make that experience tolerable is of central importance.

Sarah's instinctive reaction to leaving her house was to grit her teeth and hold her breath, and she wanted to know why these actions could not be considered tools of rote and why they seemed to make things worse rather than better. The answer, of course, is that they are merely physical expressions of her fear, part of her reaction itself rather than a conscious effort to distract herself from her fears. Another person whose instinctive reaction was different might have been helped by breathing exercises, and gritting one's teeth is not very different from chewing gum, which has proved helpful to some people. It was important for Sarah to try something different precisely because what she was in the habit of doing plainly did not work. While practicing she discovered that two or three actions seemed to help, although their effect was so limited at first she could not be sure:

a. Walking *toward* the animal (a puppy at first) rather than away gave her a feeling of control, however brief, and lessened her anxiety.

b. Similarly, calling out to the animal helped, and so did stomping a foot if it came too close.

c. Snapping her fingers softly until the animal turned its attention elsewhere.

Since after a while Sarah came to believe in exposure therapy, she was not surprised that these measures practiced over and over again were able to control her anxiety and ultimately dissipate her phobia. What surprised her came later. One day without warning she was invited from the audience to speak to a woman's group about her porcelain collection. She was immediately panicky, as, perhaps, someone who was not truly phobic might also have been. She felt the same strange physical feelings and the same sense of impending loss of control that used to overcome her when she spied a cat staring at her from behind a bush. As she walked to the podium almost by habit she began to snap her fingers—and promptly the panic receded, as if it were an animal she was about to confront instead of a roomful of women!

Knowing these truths, the phobic situations you have yet to confront will seem not much different from those you have already overcome. Consequently, the rate at which you progress from one to another accelerates. A seemingly new task, such as driving in an automobile to a resort a few hundred miles away, will be seen as only a small extension of the accustomed task of driving nearby over a familiar highway.

5. If the areas where you must practice are very far from home, condense two or three practice sessions into one. This makes practicing possible and provides the additional

benefits described earlier that come from extended periods of practice. Do not be surprised if a particular phobic situation you have been dreading for years fails to evoke any anxiety at all. On the other hand, do not be discouraged if you must suddenly cope once again with a panic attack in a place where you have not felt anxious in months. Such is the nature of the condition. It reminds you from time to time that it has not yet gone away completely.

FEELINGS TO COPE WITH AT THIS STAGE: depression and boredom.

STAGE EIGHT: FINISHING TREATMENT

Typically, the phobic who is almost all better reserves one or two places or circumstances that he will not confront.

"People who are not phobic also avoid the subways, you know," they say.

Or, "I never have occasion to drive over bridges."

Or, "It seems silly to take a plane trip just because I'm afraid of taking a plane trip."

These are excuses. It is as if the phobic, who may have led a circumscribed life for years, is hesitant to become completely free, afraid of what true freedom may represent. Or, having come to treatment with modest expectations, he may feel content simply to have achieved those goals. Such a person is suffering a failure of imagination. He cannot picture himself living a truly independent and adventuresome life. To be calm is his principal ambition. Being calm is no little thing to someone who has been miserably anxious much of the time, but much more is within reach. After all, life is supposed to be fun, which means meeting new people and doing new things—spontaneously, without concern for imaginary dangers. In any case, no accommodation short of a full recovery is stable. As long as someone is afraid of becoming panicky in some particular place, he is still afraid of the panic itself. Unless he persists long enough to become entirely better, he may at some future point respond to an anxious feeling by becoming phobic all over again.

April had been claustrophobic for many years before entering treatment. Her fears were of beauty parlors, restaurants, and other closed-in places. But, like everyone suffering from one form or another of agoraphobia, what she was really afraid of was her own feelings spiraling out of control. In other words, her phobia had grown out of a panic disorder.

She threw herself energetically into treatment, progressing slowly but steadily. By using tools she found she could tolerate most situations. Within a few months she was going almost everywhere, avoiding only one particularly noisy and crowded restaurant.

"I don't like the place very much," she said by way of explanation, "and it's not very convenient. I don't see why I have to go there even once."

But when pressed she admitted the real reason she stayed away was her fear that in those particularly cramped and crowded circumstances she might once and for all become so panicky she would at last lose control of herself and create a scene. She said that she knew "the theory" well enough and did not need to put herself to the test everywhere. The fact was she was still afraid of becoming panicky.

Over the next few months she continued to do well, going places readily and remaining there comfortably. Then one day without warning and without apparent reason she came with her husband and friends to the door of a new restaurant and found to her surprise that she could not enter. This new restaurant, perhaps because it was busy, reminded her of that other restaurant she had never mastered. Very soon her fear generalized to all restaurants, and her phobia had returned.

Knowing "the theory" is not enough. In order to get well completely April had to know that she would never lose control of herself *no matter how difficult the circumstances.* To know that, she had to be willing to risk becoming panicky whatever the circumstance. At this late stage in treatment she had to desensitize herself to restaurants all over again. Although the process took less time the second time around, it was not until she had dined repeatedly in that most difficult restaurant that she became confident she could manage unfailingly in any restaurant or, indeed, any other situation. Only then could she feel certain the phobia would never return. The fear of a panic attack or the attack itself on those rare occasions when it did recur could no longer deter her.

April might well have become worse. Had she refrained from entering once again into situations frightening to her, she might well have become housebound despite all her previous struggles to get well. On the other hand, had she not delayed for so long overcoming her phobias once and for all, this abrupt worsening of her condition could not have taken place. *When the phobic is no longer afraid of getting panicky anywhere, no matter what the circumstances, his condition can be said to be cured.* Even then, unpredictably and infrequently, short-lived panic attacks will occur. Only after a period of years are they gone forever.* These residual attacks make little impression. They are readily managed with the tools the patient has come to rely on during therapy, but later on most phobics—now exphobics—simply turn their attention elsewhere. It is as simple as that. They turn back to the ordinary matters from which they were distracted a moment before. The strange feelings that are the panic attack come just as suddenly and when they do come are still sharp and still inexplicable, usually; but they have lost the power to frighten. The task of this stage of treatment, therefore, is to make sure there is *no* place you cannot go simply because you are afraid of what you might feel when you get there.

---

* See Chapter 8 for an exception. When panic attacks occur as a facet of an agitated depression, they may return in the future when and if the depression returns.

INSTRUCTIONS

1. Do not avoid any place or set of circumstances because of the phobia. A panic attack will not incapacitate you no matter what you are doing, no matter where you happen to be. A very few endeavors will suffer from extreme anxiety—a musical performance or an important examination, for example—but even then not usually to any considerable extent. In any case, the only way to cope with such "stage fright" is to engage in that particular activity repeatedly until it becomes somewhat accustomed. Those medications that temporarily reduce anxiety to a more satisfactory level may interfere with performance because of their other effects. This is more a problem of professional performers than of people prone to panic attacks. Certainly no ordinary activity such as driving an automobile will be impaired significantly by anxiety.

If you are afraid of a particular place because you think it is truly dangerous—such as the subway, even though two or three million people ride on it every day—then you should not go there. Do not ride the subway. But if you know very well that you avoid it because in that setting you feel trapped or anxious for any other irrational reason, then there is no alternative to riding the subway. You should ride it until it no longer matters to you whether you ride it or not. Then you can stop. At this late stage of treatment two or three rides are usually enough. A similar rule can be set down for every sort of phobia. Someone afraid of heights should not stop short of going into a tall building, indeed, the tallest building around. Someone afraid of traveling should not delay indefinitely making that single, prolonged trip he has always dreaded, whether it is to a relative in another state or to Europe. Of course it is not always possible to put everything aside to take a trip to Europe, but these final confrontations should be undertaken as soon as possible. They often prove to be anticlimactic. Having dealt with your anxious feelings over and over again, you may find yourself more or less calm during these ultimate trials. You may no longer be phobic, but until you go past the last obstacles, you cannot be sure. Is it necessary for someone afraid of heights to throw himself out of a plane skydiving or, short of that, climb a mountain? No. These are activities far removed from ordinary life. They are potentially dangerous or likely at least to become unpleasant for reasons having nothing to do with a phobia. Similarly, one need not drive on icy roads, walk through bad neighborhoods, hang out a window, hurtle up and down a roller coaster, handle poisonous snakes, juggle on television, or ride in a submarine. However, do not try to convince yourself that there is a danger looming in front of you when you really know there is none.

2. Try to get panicky! In a way this is what you have been doing all along. By entering into phobic situations, getting panicky, and remaining to deal with those feelings, you counter the basic causes of the phobia: the fear of being overwhelmed and the urge to withdraw. Early in treatment, or before treatment has begun, you may have been able to frighten yourself just by imagining yourself in the phobic situation. You could feel peculiar just by thinking, "What if I begin to feel peculiar?" But no longer. The panicky experience is by now so attenuated and so plainly without implication, you cannot get panicky simply by an effort of will or imagination, no more than you can frighten yourself by the thought of being buried alive. The fantasy is too bizarre, the likelihood too remote to take seriously. In order to get panicky at this stage you may have to go further into unfamiliar situations than you ever thought would be possible. If indeed you *cannot* get panicky no matter what you do, you may be well along to a cure. Even so, you will surely get panicky spontaneously once again sometime in the future. Count on it. It is in the nature of the condition.

3. Try to get lost! Get into a car and drive a distance by yourself down unfamiliar roads. Enjoy the trip if you can. Then find your way home. Look at a map, if you like, and by all means ask directions. This is not an exercise in survival techniques but a simple demonstration of what everyone else already knows: In this day and age of sprawling cities and interconnecting highways, it is impossible to get lost for more than a few minutes at a time. Nor is it possible to be truly alone when a telephone is never more than a few feet away. The fear of getting lost or finding yourself forever alone must be seen once and for all for what it is: an illusion.

4. Whatever crutches you have used in the past, try to do without them now. If you have been carrying around a can of soda in case you should choke or a paper bag in case you should hyperventilate, leave it behind. You never needed these things in the first place. If you have managed to drive places by calling people from time to time on a CB radio, stop using the radio. If you have been calling someone on the telephone before going to see him—in case you should become incapacitated along the way and need help—now is the time to prove to yourself that you can manage all by yourself. You may feel more comfortable giving up these devices a little at a time, for example, by substituting a small can of juice for a can of soda, then liquid-filled candies for the juice. More often, just putting them aside all at once is easiest. Medication, unless it is needed for some other purpose, should also be put away. Even the list of tools you have been carrying with you can be discarded. If you get panicky, the tools you are accustomed to will come readily to mind. After a while even these become unnecessary. You will do then simply what anyone else does in the face of a distraction: Turn your attention back to the business at hand. If there is still some place you can go only with a helper, now is the time to go there by yourself. You can keep in touch with your helper indefinitely, as you

would with any other friend, and if you experience a set-back, you may need to use him again for a while; but in the end you must be free to do whatever anyone else can do with no more help than anyone else needs—which is not to say without any help at all. We are, none of us, so independent we do not rely on others all the time. But we need them as people, not as someone simply to stand nearby.

5. Become a helper. It is not necessary to be entirely re-covered before becoming a phobia aide. Because someone is depending on you, naturally you can no longer withdraw impulsively from a phobic situation. To be an aide you need to have reached that point where you are certain you can remain. You can feel certain, however, if you have lasted through a dozen or so panic attacks without running away. Everyone feels uneasy the first time he works with a pa-tient. "What if" thinking now takes the form of imagining the awful embarrassment should you need to run out of a department store or restaurant while someone else is counting on you to distract him from his own anxious feel-ings. In real life, no such thing seems to happen. Faced with a real responsibility, phobics and ex-phobics are very reliable. You may very well become anxious, but it is ex-ceedingly unlikely you will run off and desert someone who needs you. Nor should you worry about *appearing* anxious. The patient who is acutely anxious and self-conscious is not likely to waste time observing you for signs of weakness. Besides, there is no reason for a helper to pretend to be calm. What matters is not that he seems impervious to stress but that he sets an example for dealing with it—by being ready to admit his anxious feelings and by coping with them in the phobic situation.

It is precisely because working as a phobia aide is de-manding that it is helpful. Having to be at a certain place at a certain time for a particular period of time—and being able to satisfy those requirements—makes plain once and for all that you can function well even when you are anxious. Or panicky. And along the way you will be a help to someone else.

6. Now, at last, is the time to plan for the future. No one can presume to say how someone else should live, so what follows are suggestions only, but they are reasonable suggestions.

Plan on not being phobic. If you make special provisions for being incapacitated, you will limit your achievements and satisfactions and at the same time make a relapse more likely. Do not insist on living within sight of your parents' home. Do not choose a job on the basis of its being nearby and "convenient." Make application for challenging jobs if they are interesting. Even if you are busy with important matters such as bringing up children, plan as soon as you can to get a job, even if only part-time. Experience indicates that phobics are less likely to become symptomatic again if they are obligated to satisfy the demands of a daily job. Do not hesitate to attend school, go on vacations, or meet new people. Do not choose your friends solely by their willingness to tolerate your canceling appointments at the last minute. Do not marry or stay married simply because you are afraid of living by yourself. In short, do not settle for a life any less satisfying than that to which everyone else aspires.

Try to be open in your relationships with others. You may not be phobic, but like the rest of us you still have weaknesses and occasional failures. Try not to hide them, for then you will be hiding from them. You cannot become the kind of person you would like to be without first accepting yourself the way you are. Try to express your feelings openly. If the panic attack represents a welling-up of unconscious impulses, expressing them in an appropriate way should lessen their severity. But saying what is on your mind should not require special justification. It is the only way others can know what you want and need. Even more important, perhaps, speaking freely is one way of finding out who you really are, and it is the final standard of true independence: being able to state your opinion and your wishes no matter who is present and no matter what they may think.

FEELINGS TO COPE WITH AT THIS STAGE: complacency and, as always, fear.

Chapter 7

THE ROLE OF THE HELPER, THE FAMILY, THE GROUP

Growth is a natural but not automatic process. In order for a child to learn how to be an adult, someone has to teach him. In order for him to develop confidence in his ability to manage the various stresses that life brings and to manage himself also, he needs to model himself on others who live confidently and successfully. Growth in this sense goes on throughout life. As indicated earlier, for most phobics this process of learning has in some subtle way gone awry. They view the world as dangerous and foreign. They see their own existence as precarious. They cope with the dangers of their existence, real or imaginary, by a strategy of withdrawal that buys a period of respite but at the cost of a heightened anxiety and a diminished readiness to deal realistically with these dangers the next time they present themselves. Since in their view every day brings with it a new chance for something to go wrong, life becomes a continual retreat. It is difficult to reverse this process and very difficult without the help of others. An important role in treatment, therefore, falls to family members and friends. They have to teach a more effective way of confronting life.

A trained phobia aide is best able to serve as helper.

Experience counts. Knowing just what to do and just when to do it comes not only from knowing the principles of treatment but also from knowing what other phobics have accomplished. What a particular phobic can do varies over time. Even the most experienced therapist can demand too much of a phobic at a time when he should instead be patient, or, more likely, he can make the opposite mistake and expect too little. Pressed too hard, the phobic suffers more discomfort than necessary and is likely to give up. Not pressed hard enough, he will become discouraged by his lack of progress. This condition is difficult to treat, and the therapist can err in a number of different directions. Someone without experience naturally feels even more uncertain about how to help. But there is no substitute for a helper. Family members have similar important roles to play, and if a group can be formed of other phobics and ex-phobics, they too can be very helpful to one another. It is best if there is a psychiatrist or some other professional with whom these different helping people can consult; but often none is available. In lieu of such ongoing supervision, I offer the following general guidelines. Much of what is said here is implicit in the preceding chapters.

INSTRUCTIONS TO A HELPER

1. *Familiarize yourself with the principles of therapy.* If the person you are trying to help is seriously phobic, he should certainly consult with a psychiatrist or psychologist. If you are going to serve as helper, you should come along for one joint session. It is desirable also that you feel free to contact the psychiatrist if you have questions from time to time about your role. You may be able to relay important information to him. You can find out more about how to help by reading this book and the other books recommended in the Appendix. There is not yet a unanimity

among professionals on every aspect of treatment. For example, some are more inclined to use medication than others. But there is a consensus about the usefulness of exposure therapy and some agreement about how it should be conducted. Adhere as closely as you can to these principles. You cannot rely on "common sense," which may mislead you. Consider these common fallacies:

"This woman has a lot of ridiculous reasons for not doing things, and I don't think she really believes any of them."

"I think if she really wanted to go places, she could just make up her mind and go."

"I think it's a waste of time to do all these halfway, in-between steps. One hard push is all it takes."

These ideas expressed forcibly to a phobic, as often they are, are demeaning, demoralizing, and destructive of any cogent attempt at treatment. And they are inaccurate.

2. *If you do not already know the phobic patient with whom you will be working, get to know him.* Because phobias—unlike most other emotional disorders—are a response to particular fears, they are amenable to a stepwise treatment program that allows patients to confront and overcome those fears a little at a time. Most patients, therefore, can be seen to pass through the same stages along the way of recovery. Their course is similar. It would be convenient if everyone could be managed successfully in exactly the same way—as one would go about tuning up any automobile engine—and it is remarkable that to a considerable extent such a methodical approach does work. If it did not, this book would serve no useful purpose. But for treatment to work most effectively, consideration must be given to the distinctive qualities of personality that make everyone a unique human being with his own particular strengths and weaknesses, and needs. These translate into quite different ways of responding to the demands of exposure therapy. As any teacher will tell you, some people learn best with close supervision, others do better on their

own. Some require constant encouragement, others are self-starting. Different people do variously better or worse if they are coaxed, cajoled, reasoned with, threatened, prodded, persuaded, scolded, or congratulated—to mention a few of the usual strategies for motivating students. Phobics have distinctive personalities no less than anyone else, and what helps one person persist in the painful business of practicing does not work so well with another person. Indeed, what is helpful to a particular patient during one stage of treatment may not be helpful or appropriate later on. There is a time for trying something new and a time for simply going over what has already been learned; a time for encouraging a special effort and a time when no amount of effort can succeed. Commonly, someone plodding through an early stage needs to be reminded how much progress he has made. Later on, when he is almost well and thinks he has made quite enough progress, he needs to be reproached for not finishing. For these reasons, the better you know the phobic person, the better chance you will have to help him, and the better he knows you, the more likely it is that he will allow himself to be helped.

3. *Discuss with the phobic what you can do to help.* Make specific arrangements with respect to the amount of time the two of you can spend practicing together in the phobic situation—at least one or two hours a week, preferably more. Mention which times you can be reached by telephone. Try not to let other matters interfere with these commitments. If you cancel appointments repeatedly, you will indicate to the phobic that you have little regard for the usefulness of what you are doing—or worse, little regard for him! Do not be late, for similar reasons. Ignoring these ordinary courtesies will sabotage any kind of treatment but is particularly upsetting to a phobic, who counts every moment he is away from a safe haven. He may not be able to wait on a strange street corner for a helper who arrives fifteen minutes late. Sometimes being late is unavoidable, of course, but there is no excuse for subjecting

a patient repeatedly to such a painful experience. If your schedule is such that you cannot count on being at a particular place at a particular time, do not offer to be a helper. In this as in all other aspects of dealing with a phobic, the paramount rule is: *Be realistic and be reliable.* Do not promise more than you can deliver. If you do, you will quickly forfeit his trust, and he will listen skeptically thereafter to everything you have to say.

Try to be fair to yourself too. If you promise to spend a matter of hours each week working with someone and are also available by telephone at other prescribed times, you are undertaking a considerable commitment. It should not extend beyond that to all hours of the day and night. Otherwise, no matter how much good will you feel initially, you will soon become resentful. Such a feeling is readily apparent to the phobic and interferes with treatment. If you feel overburdened, you may give up the role of helper prematurely. Come to a general understanding with the patient ahead of time as to how long you expect to serve in that role. It is not possible to know exactly how long treatment will take, but you should not feel you are signing on indefinitely. Besides, specific goals are an encouragement to work seriously.

Exactly how you can help is made plain in the following paragraphs. However, both you and the person you are assisting should understand from the beginning that you cannot do for him what he must take responsibility for himself. You cannot worry for him, convince him of what you already know, or decide for him what he is capable of doing on any particular day. You cannot make him do what he refuses to do. Most important of all, you cannot practice for him. Indeed, if he does not practice every day, necessarily the majority of time without you, he will not be practicing enough. All you can do is help.

4. *Help the phobic patient plan practice sessions.* The phobic should draw up a list of situations that are frightening to him, ordered in a hierarchy, as indicated in previous

chapters. Plan with him daily practice sessions designed to introduce him systematically into those situations, beginning with the least threatening. It is important that these initial trials not be too painful. For that reason the transition from one task to more difficult ones should be accomplished slowly. The phobic patient will have a number of bad moments along the way of treatment; that much is unavoidable. He will be anxious to some extent. But most of the time he should be feeling not much worse than usual, and sometimes better. He should discover this fact for himself as soon as possible. Slow but consistent progress is the goal. If even these first few modest practice sessions prove too difficult or too uncomfortable, a less threatening task should be devised. Getting started is probably the hardest part of treatment.

Once practicing has begun, however, succeeding practice sessions should be made more difficult, even if only slightly more difficult. This process should be continued patiently and steadfastly. By advancing in such a way, in small increments, noticeable progress will be made from week to week until finally there is no phobic situation—no place or set of circumstances—that remains inaccessible. It does not matter how long the process takes as long as it is not so slow that the patient becomes discouraged. It is not crucial that each week's plan be fulfilled, but it is important that a plan be made. Specific goals have to be kept in mind. Otherwise, every patient tends to repeat the same task endlessly, waiting in vain to feel completely comfortable before moving forward.

The phobic may feel panicky a few days in a row; he may feel no levels of anxiety at all on other days. Both extremes are inevitable, and experiencing both are useful. Sooner or later the phobic must get panicky in order to learn how to cope with being panicky; but there must be times also of relative calm, or treatment becomes intolerable. The guiding principle is: Go as fast as possible without going so fast the phobic becomes miserable and no longer wants to practice at all! *He is the best judge of what he can or cannot do.* A proper pace requires a moderate level of anxiety during most practice sessions. If day after day the phobic is panicky most of the time, he is probably going too fast and trying to do too much. If day after day he is not at all anxious, he is not really practicing. *Occasional forays into very difficult phobic situations do not substitute for these systematic practice sessions.*

In summary:

Practice sessions should be planned ahead of time. They should take place daily and last at least an hour.

It is not necessary for the patient to adhere slavishly to these plans, but a serious attempt should be made every day to come as close to fulfilling them as possible.

Meaningful progress can take place slowly and in very small increments as long as the patient persists.

5. *Help the phobic choose tools to lower his level of anxiety.* For each phobic situation there are tools of rote and tools of concentration that are appropriate. These are things the phobic can do to occupy his attention for a moment or two, ideally for a minute or two. A partial list of such tools is included in the Appendix of this book. Anyone with imagination can make up his own list. You can help with this choice. With the patient's assistance draw up such a list, or lists, which he can carry around with him. Encourage him to use it. Remember that at the beginning of treatment few phobics have confidence in their ability to turn aside panicky feelings with these "tricks." Their inclination is to enter the phobic situation clenching their fists and gritting their teeth. This is the hard way.

The process of choosing tools is trial and error, and no particular tool is likely to work better than any other. If you are an ex-phobic or trained phobia aide, do not limit the patient to those tools that you have found most helpful in your previous experience. What usually works best is what seems to him likely to work best. Remind him, though, that the usefulness of tools—and, indeed, the benefits in general of exposure therapy—become apparent only as time goes on.

6. *Accompany the person you are helping into the phobic situation.* The fear of being alone—helpless and alone, or out of control and alone—often underlies phobic thinking, although sometimes it may be justified in rational terms:

"I need somebody next to me, so if I pass out, he can get me to a hospital."

"If I suddenly can't drive anymore, someone else can take the wheel."

It is a primitive, irrational fear having little to do with these conscious concerns. Frequently the presence of an infant is enough to allay this fear! Consequently, phobics can go places accompanied by a helper that are otherwise too threatening. When they have spent enough time in such a place, it becomes accustomed, even if someone else has been coming along. Then an additional adjustment has to be made by the phobic in order to go there by himself, but going first with someone else paves the way.

When you accompany a patient into such a place:

a. Try to be calm. The phobic can speak convincingly of the imminence of danger, perhaps an impending heart attack or an uncontrollable impulse to do something reckless. If you have come to know him well, you will recognize these dangers as imaginary. Remind him that fears of this sort are part of the phobic state and are not supported by his own medical history, if such is the case, or by any of his past behavior.

b. Be patient. Because you have had the same discussion about the supposed threat represented by a particular phobic situation a dozen times before and made the same reassuring explanation each time, do not shrink from making it one more time. A phobic has good emotional reasons for believing that he is in danger. Only prolonged experience will convince him that there is none, and only then will the explanation you give make good sense to him. In the meantime you reassure primarily by your presence and demeanor. Do not accuse the phobic of being willfully obtuse—or worse, unmotivated. Every phobic wants to get better. He wants to understand the world the way it really is and live as freely as everyone else. His emotional and physiological reaction is *automatic* and will change slowly. If he cannot participate at all in a practice session, he is probably being asked to do too much or is at a stuck point. In either case, the next practice session should have more modest goals. You may be able to conceive "in-between" steps that do not occur to him.

c. Be active. The more you can engage the phobic in conversation or in a detailed observation of his own behavior, the less he will be preoccupied by the rising sense of panic. Ask him about his levels of anxiety. Teach him to fill out charts measuring the rise and fall of those levels. These should be done in the phobic situation. They are a tool of concentration. Draw his attention to the circumstances of the phobic situation. He can keep in touch with reality by watching and listening to other people, sometimes literally by touching things. Do not tell him to "relax" or "focus on pleasant thoughts." Make suggestions about what he can *do*. Controlling behavior is easier than controlling thoughts or feelings. Show by your own example how he can talk to nearby strangers, take detailed notes, or otherwise act upon his environment, rather than wait passively for his feelings to overcome him.

d. Be encouraging. A phobic tends not to give himself credit for the small successes that are the basic elements of exposure therapy. Underline these achievements. Progress is readily discernible even early in treatment to someone looking for it. Remind the patient that phobic disorders are very similar from one person to the next, and others have managed to get well, even after being phobic for years. Try to find some modest goal for the phobic to attempt even on bad days so that he can realistically feel he is making progress. If he becomes so panicky during a practice session that he can no longer remain in the phobic situation, encourage him to stay a moment longer and go a little bit further before leaving.

7. *Review the practice sessions.* At least once a week, review the patient's most recent practice sessions, including those at which you were not present. Find out what he was thinking and doing at those times when his level of anxiety was rising and falling. Go over the charts and notes he has made. You are looking for certain characteristic ideas that provoke a panic attack. The examples of "what if" thinking the patient demonstrates should be pursued to their logical conclusion, no matter how fanciful or unlikely they seem:

"It's not going to happen, but, all right, what *would* you have done if you got so mixed up you forgot your way home?"

"Okay, for the sake of argument, what do you think *would* have happened if you had to stop the car because you couldn't drive?"

Seemingly desperate circumstances become not so threatening when they are examined realistically.

In your review you want to determine which tools or other changes in the environment have worked best to lower the phobic's level of anxiety. Usually these will continue to work, and you can recommend similar activities in the future.

Careful review is also the only way you can make sure the phobic is practicing every day. If he is not, the reasons need to be explored. Being "too busy" is not an adequate excuse and indicates that some other problem is getting in the way. What deters practicing is usually an unwarranted and exaggerated fear that it will prove too painful and, in the end, useless. Remind the patient of the high stakes: Success may mean an extended period of discomfort but also a free and independent life, so that he can go wherever he wants and do whatever he wants, free also eventually of inordinate anxiety and panic. Without treatment—which means practicing regularly—a serious phobia is likely to continue indefinitely, causing much more distress over the long run. Success is likely with proper treatment. Point out to him that practicing properly does *not* require that he be miserable most of the time, although there are miserable moments.

He may not believe you, any more than he is likely to take the assurances I offer in this book at face value. "How can I get used to doing something I can't even do the first time?" he asks. The proper reply is: "You don't have to do it. You just have to *start* doing it. A few steps into the phobic situation—a few moments—are enough."

It is not possible to command belief, but you can encourage the phobic to find out for himself that his fears, no matter how extreme or pervasive, can be conquered a little bit at a time.

If there is a real reason for an inability to practice in a particular phobic setting, explore with the patient the possibility of practicing elsewhere. In the end he will need to go everywhere, but along the way one phobic situation is as good as another. Anywhere he feels trapped and uncomfortable is a suitable place to practice.

Sometimes, following a practice session, the phobic may feel as if he has failed because he did not go as far as he had planned. This is not a failure. The next time he may go further. The only true failures are not starting at all or withdrawing at the *first* sign of panic. He may also feel that he "embarrassed" himself, "lost control," or became "hysterical." Usually what happened was nothing of the kind. He may have had trouble concentrating and seemed adrift. Unfortunately, it may turn out he left the phobic situation abruptly, so that people may have noticed. Rarely, a phobic may cry while panicky. None of these behaviors is ridiculous or reflects a "weakness"—even assuming that revealing a weakness is embarrassing or shameful, which of course it is not. By asking how other people who were present reacted to these "outbursts," you can usually demonstrate that nobody's opinion of the phobic person went down as a result of whatever happened. In fact, most of the time the lapse of capability that concerns the phobic, whatever it was—"My mind wandered and my voice started to shake"—has plainly evaded everyone else's notice! *You can help, therefore, to correct the phobic's misperceptions.* Seen through your eyes, the world is less threatening, the illness less hopeless, and the patient himself neither ridiculous nor incompetent.

8. *Help find a way past stuck points.* During the course of exposure therapy, the phobic will encounter a number of especially difficult places or circumstances into which, no matter how hard he tries, it seems he cannot go; and treatment may founder at this point. The methods by which these obstacles are overcome are illustrated in some detail in the previous chapter. The basic principles are straightforward:

a. What can be done to minimize the patient's discomfort should be done:

· Make clear to him that he is *not* committed to finishing whatever trial he has begun.
· Help him plan graceful exits should they become necessary.
· Help him to use appropriate tools to lower his level of anxiety.
· Help him arrange some reward or pleasurable activity at the end of these particularly difficult trials.

b. Find in-between steps by which the phobic can approach and then pass through the stuck point. Since you are not caught up with his "what if" fantasies or his embarrassment at having to go places only a little bit at a time, you may be able to conceive intermediate steps that would not occur to him. Keep in mind that *very small* advances from day to day are enough to get past any stuck point. In general, systematic daily practice sessions in which the phobic plods further and further into the phobic situation are much more helpful than weekly sallies to distant and very difficult places, especially when these excursions are separated by five or six days of doing nothing.

Almost certainly these in-between steps will require your participation. At first you may need to stand alongside the person you are helping as he observes the phobic situation from a relative distance, and even later on as he enters into the situation. You should then consider yourself on a lengthening tether, standing farther and farther away. What he manages with you beside him, he should practice later on with you a few feet away, then within hailing distance, then farther away but within sight, then, perhaps, around a corner but within walking distance, then by himself but with you standing by at the other end of a telephone. Sometimes a few of these intermediate steps can be skipped, and the phobic will suddenly be past the stuck point. Sometimes there is no shortcut. Every tiny advance, then, must be pursued relentlessly and tediously.

9. *Do not get in the way of the phobic's recovery.* As suggested above, there is much a helper can do to facilitate exposure therapy. Sometimes that contribution is crucial, but there are pitfalls to avoid:

Do not pretend to know more than you do. Remember, most phobics have good reasons to be skeptical. Most of them have been misinformed, repeatedly misdiagnosed, frightened unnecessarily, reassured unrealistically, and misled in many other ways. The surest way to lose the phobic's trust is to tell him something that turns out to be wrong. If he has physical symptoms, even those readily recognizable by the description in this book as due to anxiety alone, do not presume on your own authority to dismiss them. If he believes anyone, it will be a trained physician. In fact, only a doctor can say for certain that a particular symptom does not reflect physical illness, however consistent it might be with a purely emotional disorder. Do not advise medical tests such as a five-hour glucose tolerance test, an electrocardiogram, echocardiogram, thyroid studies, or hair analyses. The medical indications for these tests or any other medical test are specific and can be determined only by someone trained to that purpose. Similarly, do not encourage the phobic to take his pulse or time his breathing. These physiological indicators change normally with anxiety and have no clinical significance. Focusing his attention on them will only make him more uncomfortable. On the other hand, if he has been told by a doctor who has conducted a proper examination that he is physically well, you can remind him of that fact.

Do not advise him about food additives, vitamins, sugars, caffeine, the proper timing or frequency of meals, or any other matters of diet. Despite the great interest demonstrated in these subjects by magazines and the lay press, there is no evidence at all that any idiosyncrasy of food intake has an effect on agoraphobia or on anxiety in general. Anecdotal reports of the effects of one or another of these are worthless, no matter how convincing they sound. If you are an ex-phobic or have served previously as a phobia aide, you may feel convinced of the importance of eating or not eating certain foods. Do not argue from your own experience when you are advising someone else. Phobics are suggestible and inclined to make connections where none exists. If encouraged, they will begin to associate panic attacks with eating certain foods in addition to being in certain places.

If the person you are trying to help is under the care of a psychologist or psychiatrist, that trained professional has to be in charge of treatment. Be guided by him. Do not allow yourself to pull in a different direction. It is reasonable when someone is not doing well in any kind of treatment for any kind of medical disorder, to suggest a second professional opinion, but that is as far as you should go. If you are at odds with the patient's therapist, the patient will feel caught between the two of you, and the chance for a successful therapy will diminish.

If the patient asks you to tell him specifically what he will experience under particular circumstances or at a particular stage in treatment, or asks you to make any other detailed prediction about what will happen to him, do not hesitate to admit that you do not know. It is rarely possible for anyone to know for sure. It is reasonable to be optimistic, but do not make exaggerated claims for therapy. The patient will be disappointed and lose confidence in you and in the whole process of treatment.

Finally, once again, do not tell the patient what he can or cannot do at any particular time. He is the best judge.

The Role of the Family *

The family is the principal resource for anyone who is phobic—as it is the principal resource for anyone at all. It provides not only economic support but every other kind of support, including warmth, friendliness, pleasure, and love. Family life is the principal social experience throughout life. The family is the matrix out of which each person grows. He comes to recognize himself as a person by seeing himself through the eyes of his family; he measures himself against their expectations. Often their aspirations for him become his own and so become part of him forever.

Because the patient's family are so close to him, they are in the best position to be helpful in the treatment of a serious phobia; yet, for just that reason, they may find being truly helpful difficult. They are too involved to be objective, and the patient may not cooperate readily. Even when someone can accept help gracefully from a therapist or from a friend, the same help coming from a member of

* This issue is dealt with at length in *Caring: Home Treatment for the Emotionally Disturbed* by Fredric Neuman, M.D. (New York: The Dial Press, 1980).

his family seems to him to be demeaning. Similarly, the therapist can point out to the patient aspects of his behavior that are inappropriate or self-defeating, but a family member saying the same things might be accused of trying to mold the patient into his own image or for his own purposes.

And yet it remains true that an interested, intact family is a tremendous asset in the treatment of any sort of emotional illness. They are with the patient most of the time. They know, without needing to inquire, how he feels and how he is spending his time. They know, usually before anyone else, whether he is improving or becoming worse. They are able to comfort him as no one else can, for they mean more to him. Their influence over him is tremendous, and he may try to become well for their sake. Of course, they can exert that influence imprudently by being arbitrary, perhaps, or unreasonable. Indeed, they can undermine treatment in all sorts of ways. But the natural inclination of families is not to interfere but to help.

The family, every family, has a purpose as a social unit: it is to protect, to teach, to comfort, to allow dependence while encouraging independence—in short, to provide a setting in which maturation can occur. A good family encourages its members to behave in effective ways, yet it encourages them to find their own ways of behaving effectively. And such an effort is precisely the function of therapy. Therefore, family members, at least some of them, come naturally to the tasks of helping.

What a family member can do may be divided into two parts. He can serve as helper, following the guidelines set forth in the previous section. This is not easy to do. He is likely to react spontaneously as a parent rather than as a teacher. For the same reason, there are parents who cannot teach their children to drive an automobile—even when they can teach a neighbor's child. With their own children they may be too impatient or the children may be too impatient. When a relative acts as helper, all the complicated aspects of family relationships—dependence, ambivalence, resentment, disappointment, guilt, concern, and sometimes a desperate love—spill over into the practice sessions, making them more highly charged than they would be ordinarily. But often there is no alternative. There may be no trained aide available. Friends may not be able to spend the amount of time required. Often the only one who will is a parent or spouse. The demeanor the family member should struggle to maintain during these practice sessions is, in one word, calm.

The second way in which family members can support treatment is more subtle but no less important. They have to *make room* in their lives for that phobic person to change. It seems that each person in a family is assigned or takes on a particular role. Once the phobic has been symptomatic for a considerable time, he is expected to be dependent, worried, and circumspect, and often passive and conciliatory. Certainly he is seen as a stay-at-home. In order for him to become assertive and independent, his family has to be willing to accept him that way.

At the time when Joan began treatment at the age of thirty for an agoraphobia that had already lasted ten years, her family expressed great concern about her.

"We want her to be happy," her mother said. "She can't go outside shopping or meeting anybody. She doesn't have a boyfriend. She got a college degree, but she can't work. It's terrible. We want her to get better."

"We want to do anything we can to help her," her father said.

And with proper treatment Joan did indeed get better steadily during the next three months. Then her progress slowed, attributable, unfortunately, to a change in attitude of her parents *which they themselves did not recognize*. At first they had cooperated fully, always encouraging her and being supportive, often serving as helper. With their patient help Joan began going everywhere in her neighborhood. She volunteered at a nearby hospital and began dating. Still anxious, she began nevertheless to drive, to travel on buses, and to go places where previously she would have felt trapped and helpless. Then simultaneously she began to look for work and to date seriously a man who lived in a nearby city.

"Of course I want you to go to work," Joan's mother explained to her, "but why does it have to be Manhattan? The subways aren't safe, neither are the streets. Suppose you get stuck in a tunnel? You'll be coming home all hours. When are you going to rest?"

"Listen, it's one thing to go out, that's terrific," Joan's father commented, "but a skiing weekend? What for? I know two guys who broke a leg skiing. Also, how are we going to reach you if something goes wrong? And a whole weekend sleeping over with someone you hardly know, is that nice?"

Joan's parents sincerely wanted her to recover from her agoraphobia, but the truly independent life that was now within her reach seemed dangerous to them, so they began to exert their considerable influence *against* further improvement. They were loving parents. They would not consciously have tried to limit her recovery or chance for happiness, but in espousing their own frightened view of the world, that is what they did. It seemed to Joan they wanted her to get halfway better but no more. "They're afraid to lose me," she said.

A grown child cannot be protected from making mistakes, failing from time to time, and getting hurt occasionally in an unsuccessful relationship. Mature and sensible people who are very circumspect also have such experiences. There is no avoiding them. Someone who has not had to cope with his share is not well equipped to deal with life. Trying to protect someone who is phobic from these ordinary stresses is being overprotective. It is more sensible to make sure to be around at those times when he does get into trouble, to assure him that disappointments and difficulties are inevitable but not important as long as he learns from them and continues to face life courageously.

INSTRUCTIONS TO FAMILY

1. *Familiarize yourself with the principles of exposure therapy.* Read all the chapters of this book, especially the previous section. There are reasons to be optimistic about treatment, so do not allow yourself to become discouraged. A long-standing, severe agoraphobia can resolve completely. Encourage the family member who is phobic to give therapy a fair trial, even if he has failed previously in other forms of treatment.

2. *Serve as helper.* Even if the phobic has a trained phobia aide working with him, you will be called on to serve as helper occasionally. The more time spent practicing, the more rapid and certain is recovery. Since the phobic person relies on you, your time and effort are especially important. When serving in the capacity of helper, though, you should struggle to behave as one and not as a parent or spouse. Put family issues to one side. Overcoming the phobia must take precedence. Try to be calm, methodical, and goal-directed. Attend strictly to the business of practicing in the phobic situation. Adhere stringently to the guidelines set forth for practicing. Do not try to be innovative. The seemingly endless record-keeping, the daily practicing, and the time-consuming step-by-step approach—more accurately, little-step-by-little-step approach—are all important, even if they do not seem so to the uninitiated.

3. *Provide a supportive environment.* Everything you do should be designed to make the phobic's recovery more likely. To begin with, try to minimize the stresses to which he is subject. Exposure therapy is inherently a stressful undertaking. There is not much you can do to lessen the

anxious moments or soften the impact of a panic attack, but you should try to make the rest of the phobic's life as uncomplicated as possible. Only to a small extent can anyone be shielded from the commonplace pressures of life, including money worries, dating problems, career decisions, and personal conflicts, among others; but to the extent you can, you should. At least do not add to these pressures by a crescendo of demands linked to his progress. For example, if he is halfway to recovery, do not suggest that he find a job the next day or move out of the house. Such remarks are not an inducement to get better but a threat. They may be perceived by the patient as a desire to sabotage treatment. One particular stress *can* be relieved by an attentive family: the sense of aloneness that is often an important part of the phobia and that becomes more threatening as the prospect of becoming truly independent takes more definite shape.

A supportive environment also means a place where someone can explore his own ambitions and develop his own values and way of living without someone else objecting, a place where he can express himself forcefully and even get angry from time to time without someone snapping back at him. Family members who are basically optimistic are naturally supportive, but the parents of phobics are very often not optimistic. As suggested earlier, they tend to be phobic themselves or vaguely and diffusely frightened—just plain nervous about everything that can go wrong in life. When it is an adult child who is in therapy, they have to make a special effort—as Joan's parents did not—to let him mature, make his own mistakes, and find his own way.

4. *Do not get in the way of recovery.* There are pitfalls that family members, no less than helpers, must avoid:

a. Do not ridicule the phobic's exaggerated fears. They are real enough to him. If he sees a danger where there is none, point out the truth—calmly.

b. Do not make little of his attempts to confront his

fears. Feeble though they may seem to you, repeated day after day, they ensure recovery.

Harriet had sought treatment for years. Since her agoraphobia did not allow her to cross the street, she was in psychotherapy only briefly when a psychiatrist consented to make home visits, and these few sessions did not prove helpful. Subsequently, however, using the Home Centered Tape Program she obtained from the White Plains Hospital Phobia Clinic, she was able to make slow but steady progress. There came a day when for the first time in eight years she managed to cross the street by herself.

"I went to the grocery store by myself today!" she told her husband that evening with justified pride.

"Big deal," he replied sarcastically, not bothering to look up from his newspaper.

It was weeks before Harriet attempted once again to leave her house.

The patient should be congratulated for each small victory. They lead one to the next and eventually to a cure.

c. Do not tell the phobic that he can do something he does not think he can do, "if only he puts his mind to it." He knows best what he can do. Be patient.

d. Do not try to motivate him by making him feel guilty. He has plenty of his own reasons to go places and do things. He should not be told he has to go some place, a wedding for example, because of an obligation to someone else.

e. Do not scold, bargain, cajole, or trick the phobic into doing more than he is prepared to do. In fact, do not at the last moment coax him into doing "a little more"— even though that strategy seems to work and he *does* do a little more. In the long run your taking charge in this way will undermine his sense of being in control. It will also be a source of conflict eventually since there will be times when he definitely will not want to practice further. On the other hand, by all means *ask* him if he wants to go a little further into the phobic situation or do a little more. The further the better.

f. Do not violate the phobic's trust.

Laurie's cousin promised to drive her through the neighborhood, taking a route that both of them had agreed to before setting out. Halfway along, however, her cousin pulled up to the curb and without any warning got out of the car!

"Be back in a minute," she said. "I have to buy a cake."

Laurie, immediately in a panic, sat frozen in the car for what seemed like forever until her cousin returned only minutes later. She remained shaken the rest of the day, but, more important, she refused to allow her cousin to drive her anywhere again. Her cousin did not quite understand why she was so angry with her.

"I went just the way I said I would, didn't I?"

Certainly, you must fulfill literally every promise you make. If you say you are going to be ten paces behind, or around the corner just out of sight, or at a particular intersection at a particular time, or in your office waiting for a telephone call, *that is where you must be!* But also you must not violate the unwritten rule against precipitating the phobic into unexpected circumstances, especially those that require waiting passively. These minor alterations in plan weigh very heavily in his experience of the phobic situation and will make him regard you as not entirely reliable in future practice sessions. In short, you will lose your usefulness.

g. Finally, do not try to arrange the phobic's life so that it is "safe." As indicated earlier, the attempt to protect him from all failure, danger, or disappointment is hopeless and in the end serves to weaken rather than protect.

These various prescriptions are not easy to follow. Just living with someone who is seriously phobic is difficult. It is painful watching someone you love compromise his life because of an irrational fear. The imaginary dangers that preoccupy him seem absurd, but no amount of argument makes that plain to him. Nor does he seem to learn from experience, so his phobia threatens to last forever. And because he, or she, cannot do certain things, your life becomes more constrained and more difficult. You have to think twice before making social arrangements or scheduling vacations. You may have to do all the shopping yourself, and the car-pooling, including chauffeuring the phobic person wherever he may need to go. And if you decide to go some place special with him, you can only go to that place if it is within his safe perimeter.

It is natural to resent these limitations and these extra responsibilities. You may feel that the phobia is being used as an excuse for selfish demands of one sort or another— demands for constant attention, for example, or the right to boss everybody around. Yet, plainly, no one would pretend to be frightened and miserable all the time just to get his own way. So you feel guilty. Most of all, you feel frustrated and confused. Then, once you are involved in his treatment, as necessarily you must be, you have to worry about whether you are doing too much or too little to help, not protecting him or over-protecting him, pushing him too hard to get well or not hard enough. Sometimes the answer is clear only after the fact, when something you said or did worked or didn't work, or made things worse. And this period of treatment may well extend past eight weeks in order for the phobic to reach full recovery.

Remember these consoling thoughts during that difficult time: Treatment does not go on forever, and, if it is successful, neither does the phobia. A patient effort put in now will free the phobic and you too from the burdens of his illness. Your contribution is important, sometimes crucial. A well-intended effort, no matter how clumsy, is worthwhile and will surely have a positive effect. If that effort seems to go unappreciated now, you can be certain that it has not gone unnoticed; some people cannot acknowledge their family's help until they have recovered once and for all.

The Role of the Group

Phobics and ex-phobics meeting together can be helpful for reasons that have already been mentioned. They encourage each other and learn from each other. Each person's success is an inducement to the others. Suggestions about practicing and, in particular, about getting past stuck points are very useful. Everyone in the group should understand, though, that it has only one purpose: to facilitate recovery from a phobia. Without professional guidance no self-constituted group can hope to deal effectively with the other emotional problems of its members; if such an attempt is made, its real purpose cannot be fulfilled. No one should suggest ways for someone else to deal with his depression or compulsive rituals or marital conflict. In short, no one should intrude into anyone else's life by offering casual advice. Perhaps it goes without saying, but everyone should be careful not to say anything that might hurt someone else's feelings.

If you are phobic and if you live in or near a city, you may be able to join a group already in existence. A number of hospitals have started phobia clinics. Others have been started by trained phobia aides. The Phobia Society of America may provide information on various treatment programs available in your geographic area. More often, unfortunately, there will be no formal group available to you. If you can, then, you should start your own.

Without question there are other phobics who live near you. It is a common disorder. Since most phobics are secretive about their condition, however, it often happens that neighbors, even close friends or relatives, share the same fears without one knowing about the other. Of course, someone will be more willing to admit to you that he has a phobia if you speak openly about your own. Also, he is more likely to enlist in a treatment program if you indicate to him that there is reason to think it might work. The first step in forming a group, then, is to find others who are phobic—and to do that you must ask. A number of groups have started after public service announcements on radio or newspaper advertisements indicating the intention to form such a group.

Most phobic groups meet once or twice a week for an hour or two. Some include family members. As in any other psychotherapeutic encounter, it is desirable to start and stop on time. Some degree of formal structure helps to make explicit the goal-centered nature of treatment and distinguish these groups from ordinary social activities. The Home Centered Tape Program, which is a recording from beginning to end of all the group meetings in an eight-week clinic, can be used as the basis around which a group can be run. A typical meeting proceeds from one person to the next. There is an agenda.

Each person describes the practice sessions he undertook since the previous meeting. This account should include the plans he made prior to each session, difficulties he encountered while practicing, and the effectiveness of the tools he used to deal with his anxiety. Finally, he should indicate the day-to-day plans he has made for the following week. Suggestions are entertained by everyone else for using new tools, for finding potential exits in new phobic situations and, in general, for dealing with stuck points. Especially important is the need to set individual goals, not only for the next few days and weeks but for the next few months. Without concrete goals people tend naturally to practice the same few tasks over and over again —*which is not really practicing at all.* The weekly meeting then degenerates into an empty recitation in which everyone tells everyone else to be optimistic, without anyone really having reason to be optimistic since no one is making progress. Remember, true progress can be measured simply by answering the following:

1. What can you do now, today, that you could not do yesterday or the day before or the week before?

2. How long can you tolerate your panicky feelings before leaving the phobic situation? Can you wait longer than you did yesterday or the day before or the week before? Can you lower your levels of anxiety with the use of tools and *without* leaving the phobic situation?

It is not crucial that goals be fulfilled, but they should be explicit. If after a few weeks or even months of meeting no progress is achieved, something is going wrong. The usual explanation is that someone is at a stuck point or is trying to cope with his anxious feelings by brute force alone, without using tools. If not led aggressively, a self-help group can have a number of people at this impasse at the same time, especially since the patients who do practice and get better eventually leave the group. Should the group continue like this for any length of time, everyone will become demoralized. Often all it takes to make such a group productive again is determining for each person what he can reasonably expect to do day by day for the next few weeks. In any case, everyone should be reminded that this is not a condition that ordinarily goes away by itself. Neither does it respond to psychological interpretation or explanation or simple encouragement. What needs to be understood can only be learned by practicing in the phobic situation.

Occasionally someone does very well in treatment but falters toward the end only because he has become attached to other members of the group and does not want to be without them. He justifies continuing to come each week by remaining symptomatic. Such a person should be encouraged to finish, otherwise his improvement may not be permanent. He can remain in the group, if he wishes, as a helper or leader.

Certain commonsense rules need to be followed in running any therapeutic group:

1. The number of people in the group should be few enough to allow everyone to speak without feeling rushed.

2. Someone who feels anxious or otherwise upset should be allowed to speak out of turn or, if he wishes, leave the group for a few minutes.

3. It is desirable to include family members in the group since they are so important to the phobic's eventual recovery. Even if the group is limited strictly to phobics, however, someone such as a friend or family member may have to accompany a new patient the first few times.

4. The meeting should start on time so no one feels he is kept waiting unnecessarily, and everyone in the meeting should, if possible, arrive on time. Missing part of the meeting means there is less opportunity to learn from the others.

5. No one person should dominate the meeting either by talking too long or by telling other people what to do.

6. Someone should lead the meeting in order to make sure that everyone has a chance to speak. In a group without a trained or professional leader, a different person can lead each time.

7. There should be a minimum of banter. It is inevitable and desirable that people in the group come to know and care about each other, but personal conversation should be reserved until after the formal portion of the meeting is ended.

8. Since phobics are often shy, easily embarrassed, and sometimes frankly depressed, everyone in the group should be gentle with everyone else.

9. Being kind should not extend to telling someone he is doing well when he is not. It would be kinder to suggest ways in which he could do better.

10. There is always an emotional interplay among people who meet together regularly. It is unavoidable. Sometimes these group psychodynamics are subtle, sometimes overt.

When there are strong feelings expressed by one member of the group toward another, they are likely to interfere with the functioning of the group and distract from its purpose. To some extent these conflicts can be minimized by everyone being alert to them and trying to stick to the business at hand—how to deal with a phobia.

Members of the group can also be helpful to one another between group meetings by acting as one another's aide and by making themselves available by telephone. Having a sympathetic and understanding friend within reach can make all the difference. Sometimes, when a particular set of circumstances is threatening to all the members, riding elevators for example, the entire group can practice together. This sort of field trip has proven especially useful in dealing with the fear of flying. Many airlines welcome the opportunity to demonstrate to groups of phobics the workings of an airplane and to attest to their safety record. Sometimes a short flight can be arranged.

Whether someone is a phobia aide, a relative of a phobic, or a member of a therapeutic group in which he participates, to some extent he is cast in the role of therapist. By caring, he exerts a special influence. This is a significant fact, since psychotherapy is essentially the influencing of one person by another.

Of course, anyone who does psychotherapy, in any sense of the word, must be concerned with the same clinical issues that are of concern to a primary therapist doing treatment. He must be alert to his patient's personal reaction to him and to the response he has in return. Such a response is unavoidable, but it should be under control, to some extent measured. The therapist must be tolerant of the patient's weaknesses but not indulgent. He must be sympathetic but also dispassionate. He must be optimistic but at the same time realistic. Finally he must have respect for the patient's symptoms. He must not expect too much improvement too fast. He must keep in mind especially that although he may intervene in his patient's life, he may not intrude. Considering these difficulties, it is remarkable that therapy works as well as it does, even in untrained hands.

Chapter 8

RELATED PROBLEMS: AGITATED DEPRESSION, REACTIVE HYPOGLYCEMIA, AND MITRAL VALVE PROLAPSE

Described in this chapter is an important illness, depression, which can cause or complicate agoraphobia, and two other illnesses, hypoglycemia and mitral valve prolapse, important only because they are associated in people's minds with phobias. All three require discussion. At this time, however, not enough is known to write with absolute certainty about any one of them or of their relationship to the panic disorder that underlies agoraphobia. What is set down here is to some extent a matter of opinion; others in the medical community have different opinions. In this respect agoraphobia is no different from most illnesses. Research usually continues for years before basic issues such as etiology and proper treatment can be resolved finally, and in a very real sense certain issues always remain in doubt. For that reason it is tempting simply to avoid writing this chapter. Then I would not risk annoying colleagues by expressing a point of view that contravenes their own experience or understates in their opinion, or overstates various lines of research and evidence. More important, I would run no risk of inadvertently misleading the phobics who read this book. More than most people, they have a need for certainty. If they have heard that a heart attack can be provoked by too much exercise, they will be uncomfortable every time they engage in a sport— no matter how unlikely such an outcome might be. But in the real world we cannot know anything for sure. We must plan our lives nevertheless. Since phobics tend to be at one and the same time suggestible yet skeptical, there is special reason for them to understand just how reliable or unreliable is the information they come to receive in various places from friends, or newspaper articles—or books such as this one. It is worth taking a few moments, therefore, to explain how someone, a phobic person or a physician, should try to determine in his own mind what is likely to be the truth.

Personal Experience

It is natural for people to judge facts of life by their own particular experiences or the experiences of others whom they know. Sometimes these ideas sum to a conventional wisdom or "common sense." One such idea is the commonly held view that going outside underdressed on a cold, wet day is likely to cause that person to catch cold. Another is the notion that children allowed to eat whatever they choose will eat an unbalanced diet—mostly junk food. Some phobics have been convinced by observing their diet that there is a relationship between the ingestion of simple sugars and panic attacks. The corresponding personal experience by which doctors guide their actions is called *clinical experience*, the sum of their various encounters with a particular illness, drug, or kind of therapy. Factored in here, also, is what the physician has learned from colleagues and teachers, and from other clinicians. Obviously, the more extensive someone's clinical experience, the more reliable his judgment—and this is also true for those who are not professionals. But, then, how can two experienced physicians differ in their judgment? How can one psychiatrist feel strongly that a particular drug ameliorates a phobia while another feels that it makes it worse? Indeed, the conventional wisdom of one time or place is contradicted by that of another. The sad fact is that personal experience is not usually very reliable. No matter how hard someone struggles to be objective, his judgment is colored by prejudice and by extraneous circumstances. He is especially influenced by what he wants to believe. Compounding this problem is the feeling everyone has that somehow he himself is immune to these unconscious influences—that he, at least, can see things the way they really are. Perhaps physicians are more prone to this conceit than others. Even in someone who is responsible and realistic, the sense of certainty is likely to overwhelm his better judgment. Worse, believing in something strongly tends to color further experience so that the belief is affirmed. This is called a self-fulfilling prophecy. Someone who *expects* to feel nervous after eating a chocolate bar may very well begin to feel nervous for that reason alone. Explainable in these terms is the well-known placebo response. If a patient is given a medication by a doctor whom he respects, he is likely to experience some relief of his symptoms, whatever they are, even if there was no active ingredient in the medicine! Such a drug is called a placebo and is used commonly to relieve pain or anxiety when tranquilizers or more conventional pain relievers might be dangerous or in some other way disadvantageous. Everyone responds to placebos to a greater or lesser extent. It is a very real, reproducible phenomenon in no way caused by or associated with emotional disorders. Placebos can even cause side effects! It is possible to have a negative placebo response. Someone told not to expect much from a medication may show little effect from it even if it would otherwise work. * How then can a doctor judge from the response of a patient or group of patients whether or not a particular drug has merit? Does this mean that all experience is useless? Of course not, but it does mean we must observe closely and with a high index of suspicion. When certain commonsense ideas are tested rigorously, they turn out to be false, including the examples given above. When a group of volunteers were soaked for a period of hours in cold water, they did *not* come down with colds any more frequently than another group who were not subjected to this unpleasant trial. A group of carefully observed children allowed to eat in a controlled setting whatever they chose, chose to eat a balanced diet. And, finally, studies have shown that for the great majority of agoraphobics, panic attacks do not correlate with blood sugar levels.

Formal Research

Science has devised techniques for investigating medical issues in ways that attempt to eliminate bias. These involve formal research protocols, including elaborate statistical analyses and double-blind studies. Such studies are an important tool invented to cope with the specific problem described earlier of determining the true value of a particular drug. A double-blind experiment is one in which half of a number of patients take the drug under study and the other half are given a placebo. Both pills look alike, and neither the patients *nor* the doctor know which patient is getting which pill. If the patients who have taken the real medicine do *significantly* better than the others, it is an

---

* A patient of mine complained that when I prescribed imipramine for her it did not block her panic attacks, although previously when it was prescribed in smaller doses by a different psychiatrist it worked! Did she respond then because she was told she would, or did she not respond now because I indicated to her that I did not expect her to?

indication that the medication has an intrinsic value over and above its placebo effect. But the issue is not resolved so simply. The term "significance" itself illustrates the ambiguities still present in these most objective scientific studies. A particular result is said to be "significant at the 5 percent level" if there is only a 5 percent chance of the result being obtained *by chance alone*. By that standard a drug may be judged to be effective. Well, that means there is indeed some chance, perhaps a one-in-twenty chance, of this seemingly useful drug having no real value at all. Similarly, a drug found not to be effective at this level of significance may very well turn out after further investigation to be effective after all. Contradictions of this sort are more the rule than the exception. Of course, the more consistent a finding from study to study and from time to time, the more confident someone can feel in the results.

As anyone who has ever done research knows, there are other reasons to be skeptical of the reports that appear in the medical literature. Despite all precautions, to some extent results are influenced by the preconceived notions of the investigator. Data that are not supportive of the experimental thesis are often somehow redefined out of consideration. There is a margin of error even in the straightforward act of reading figures off a meter, and this error and similar ones tend to be made always one way rather than the other. Sometimes the safeguards built into double-blind studies vanish in practice. For example, the side effects of antidepressants (drugs frequently prescribed to block panic attacks) are so obvious—a dry mouth and sweating, among other easily recognizable symptoms —it is often apparent both to the patient and to his doctor that he is taking that drug and not the control substance. What all this means is that the results of published studies cannot be relied on absolutely any more than personal experience.

Having made this elaborate apology for not having all the answers, I feel obligated nevertheless to express a clear opinion on the three medical conditions discussed in this chapter. This opinion is based on considerable personal experience and careful reading of the medical literature, some of which is in conflict, but it is not the final word. Nor is anyone else in the position now to offer the final word—however definite he may sound.

If you are concerned, as very many phobics are, that you are suffering from one of these conditions, you should learn as much as you can about it. The first place you should go for information is to your doctor. In recognition that many people remain in doubt, though, I present at the end of this chapter a representative bibliography drawn from the medical literature. These articles are not easy to read by someone who is untrained, but for the most part they are comprehensible. At least their gist is clear. Phobics tend to frighten themselves reading the distorted accounts in the popular literature of one disease or another, usually focusing on some catastrophic although rare complication, but these fears grow out of knowing too little about the illness, not knowing too much. Knowing the truth—insofar as it is possible to know the truth—is almost unfailingly reassuring.

Agitated Depression

There is a well-recognized overlap between depression and panic disorder leading to agoraphobia. The families of severe phobics show a higher incidence of depression than would be expected otherwise, suggesting a genetic relationship. The phobics themselves are often depressed, sometimes severely; a careful history often reveals that the phobia began when the patient suffered a so-called endogenous depression. Not all depressions are alike. Some are more severe than others. Some are acute, others chronic. Some cause lethargy, others agitation—or a variety of other symptoms. Some are reactive; that is, in response to a difficulty in the person's life, usually a loss. Others are endogenous, meaning coming from within. This last condition has special relevance to the development of agoraphobia and explains, I think, the reported success of various antidepressant medication in diminishing or blocking panic attacks.

An endogenous depression is marked not only by the pervasive sadness and the regretful or discouraged thoughts that characterize every sort of depression but by vegetative signs. These are disturbances of bodily function. The most important is a derangement of sleep in which the person falls asleep readily but wakes up during the night, often with nightmares, then wakes up again in the early hours of the morning unable to get back to sleep and miserable. When this pattern is reproduced day after day for a period of weeks, it is a strong indication of a depression. Typically, there is also a diurnal variation of mood in which, if the depression is not too severe, the miserable feeling wears off slowly during the course of the day. Finally, there is a loss of appetite to the point of losing weight. There may be a variety of other symptoms, including physical complaints. These need not be explained here. What is important to know is that these depressions sometimes cause an agitation that is indistinguishable from a panic attack. When that sense of restless nervousness recurs day after day, as it usually does, often from the moment of waking up, the affected person may respond, as phobics do, by remaining home, away from work or from other social situations. Different places seem suddenly threatening, and so does remaining home alone, so that he may insist that someone remain home with him. Indeed, this is often how a phobia begins. An untreated depression may last many months, and by the time it has gone a pattern of avoidance and fearfulness has developed that continues with a life of its own. Although the constant state of agitation is gone now, remaining behind are occasional sudden bursts of anxiety—in other words, panic attacks—which come on in part because they are remembered and feared, and expected. This is not the usual onset of a severe phobia, but it is not at all uncommon.

Someone in the throes of an agitated depression will respond the great majority of times to antidepressant drugs. His anxiety, restlessness, and panicky feelings will *not* be relieved solely by engaging in exposure therapy. The medication is essential. If medical treatment of his depression is delayed long enough for agoraphobia to develop, he should be regarded as having both illnesses. The depression must be treated first. Being very depressed makes it impossible for most people to function in any setting, let alone practice in the phobic situation. Someone who does have the courage and stubbornness to practice every day despite such a feeling is wasting the effort. The tools he uses will *not* lower his level of anxiety, and he will not find himself able to go further and further into the phobic situation. Eventually he will come to believe that treatment is without effect. Actually, exposure therapy works very well for these patients—relieving anticipatory anxiety and avoidance behavior and allowing for control of the panic attacks themselves—but only after the depression has lifted, either with medication or of its own accord after a prolonged period of time. In short, antidepressant drugs should be prescribed and exposure therapy should be put off a few weeks until the depression has receded. By then the patient is likely to be sleeping well, feel fine most mornings, eat well—sometimes too well—and be generally optimistic. In my experience the panic attacks still persist and are still troublesome, although greatly reduced in number. * The phobia itself—namely, the wish to avoid certain situations in order to avoid the sense of being trapped or helpless—is likely to remain also, but not always.

---

* As indicated earlier, other physicians report a more encouraging experience for a number of reasons, some of which have been suggested above.

So much is straightforward, but there is a complicating factor: An agitated depression need not be present with all of the classical features described above. In particular, not everyone suffering from an agitated depression reports that he is feeling depressed! Not infrequently the agitation and feeling of anxiety predominate. The affected person may be under the impression that he is depressed only as a consequence of feeling restless, frightened, and just plain terrible all day long—rather than the other way around. For this reason many patients, and physicians too, are under the impression that the illness they are trying to cope with is an uncomplicated agoraphobia manifested primarily by constant panic attacks. It is the inclusion of this group of patients in studies of the drug treatment of agoraphobia that accounts, I think, for the apparent effectiveness of antidepressant drugs "blocking" panic attacks.* The fact is, an agitated depression, like every other medical illness, can be present in individual patients with certain features more prominent than others.

Whether or not a patient reports himself explicitly as depressed, he should be offered a trial of antidepressant drugs under the following circumstances:

1. The presence of severe anxiety occurring every morning immediately upon arising and lasting intermittently for hours. Phobic patients who do *not* have a complicating depression wake up occasionally very anxious on days when they must confront an especially difficult challenge, such as taking an airplane flight, but all the rest of the time they wake up feeling fine.

2. The presence of "panic attacks" that last hours instead of minutes and that recur every day whether or not the individual is in a phobic situation.

* If the study group is large enough, the inclusion of a small percentage of patients who almost always respond to one form of treatment (drugs) and almost never to another kind (exposure therapy) will cause the overall study to show a statistically "significant" advantage to the first kind of treatment. This would be true even if all the rest of the group, perhaps 80 percent to 90 percent, show no benefit at all from that treatment.

3. Finally, and most important, the presence of the vegetative signs of depression:

    a. Persistent early-morning awakening

    b. A diurnal variation of mood, worse in the morning and becoming somewhat better during the course of the day

    c. Loss of appetite to the point of losing weight

These symptoms are usually accompanied by sadness, irritability and the other subjective complaints of depression; even when they are not, if they continue without relief for a period of weeks, they are an indication of an underlying endogenous depression. In response to sufficient amounts of medication prescribed over a long enough period of time, all of these symptoms disappear. However, if the patient is phobic too, he will still get panicky from time to time and will still hesitate to enter into phobic situations. He will need then to enter into exposure therapy. It is likely he will benefit from it. If he goes through all the stages of recovery, the phobia should not return in the future; however, the depression might. If so, it will respond each time to the same drugs.

It should be understood that the usual route to agoraphobia is *not* by way of an agitated depression. Most people who are phobic do *not* have the symptoms listed above. For that reason most severe phobics are not, unfortunately, improved solely by the use of antidepressant drugs, at least in my experience. *

Reactive Hypoglycemia

Hypoglycemia means low blood sugar. It is not an illness but simply a physical finding. It can be caused by a number of conditions of varying seriousness, and in turn it

---

* For a different experience see G. Houshang, et al. "Treatment of Panic Disorder with Imipramine Alone," *American Journal of Psychiatry*, Vol. 141, No. 3 (March 1984): 446–48.

can cause a variety of symptoms which seem at first glance to resemble those of a phobia. These include lightheadedness, shakiness, sweating, weakness and fatigue, nervousness, fast heart beat, blurring of vision, and tingling of lips and tongue, among others. They are relieved promptly by raising the blood sugar to the proper levels. The terms "reactive hypoglycemia" or "functional hypoglycemia" are used vaguely to refer to a condition in which someone for undiscovered or undiscoverable reasons overreacts to the ingestion of sugars by a rise and then an abrupt fall in blood sugar levels, precipitating the symptoms listed above. There is some doubt about whether such a condition exists at all. There is no question that the great majority of times the diagnosis is made, it is made in error. Anxious people (often phobics who are concerned about the possibility of suffering some obscure physical illness) come to the attention of a careless physician who performs a glucose tolerance test and without further investigative procedures informs the patient he has hypoglycemia, which will have to be treated by eating five or six meals a day for the rest of his life. Or the patient may be self-diagnosed, matching up his symptoms with those described for hypoglycemia. Or he may have become convinced he is hypoglycemic from listening to a friend who is recommending the disease to everyone. There are *societies* of people who feel they are hypoglycemic and who recommend a hypoglycemic diet to *everyone* who feels anxious. The conviction some people have that they are hypoglycemic rises to delusional proportions and persists in the face of any amount of contrary evidence. They discount repeated blood sugar tests in the normal range, despite their being obtained at times when "hypoglycemic" symptoms are present. "I know what I feel, and I can see for myself," they insist. * It is very difficult to help these people overcome their phobias since

* This is a startling example of the unreliability of subjective experience— and also, perhaps, of the need to find a simple concrete explanation for a complicated psychological condition.

they attribute their condition not to a mistaken understanding of themselves and of the world but rather to a physiological state. In that case there is nothing to learn from practicing. Yet despite their diet, they still have panic attacks and remain phobic.

True hypoglycemia is complicated and beyond the scope of this book. The reader is directed to the medical bibliography at the end of the chapter and to the various books written on the subject by endocrinologists.* Certain salient points should be made, though:

1. The diagnosis of hypoglycemia cannot be made by observing one's symptoms subjectively and relating them to diet. It is too easy to be led astray.

2. The five-hour glucose tolerance test was not designed to test for hypoglycemia, and it is not very useful for that purpose. The test is inconsistent from laboratory to laboratory and from time to time, depending in part on what the patient ate during the two or three days prior to the test and on how long the blood is allowed to stand in the test tube. (With time, the sugar level drops falsely as much as 30 percent.) Finally, the test itself provokes low blood sugar unnaturally by requiring ingestion of pure sugar after a period of prolonged abstinence from food. This is *not* an ordinary diet.

3. Fifty percent of *normal* people will run a blood sugar below 70 milligrams per deciliter at times. Healthy men who have been fasting for three days often reach levels in the low 50s without experiencing symptoms or showing any signs of bodily dysfunction. During the course of a glucose tolerance test, 25 percent of normal people are found to have a level below 50 mgm/dl. If during the tests their level is monitored continuously, 42 percent are below 50 mgm/dl. The level of fasting blood sugar strongly suggestive of hypoglycemia is below 40 mgm/dl, although a higher level between 40 and 60 mgm/dl. is a "gray zone"

---

* In particular read Lynn Bennion, M.D., *Hypoglycemia: Fact or Fad* (New York: Crown Publishers, 1983).

consistent under certain circumstances with hypoglycemia. In order to make the diagnosis properly, however, these levels must regularly produce the symptoms described above, and each time when the level of blood sugar is raised, the symptoms should disappear.

4. In fact, the diagnosis of hypoglycemia should be pursued in the first place by repeated determinations of blood sugar levels *at those times when the patient is experiencing symptoms.* It is these readings that are important, rather than the results of a glucose tolerance test. Tested in such a way, the great majority of phobic patients can quickly assure themselves they do *not* have this additional problem.

5. Finally, when hypoglycemia *is* present, it is vitally important to discover its cause. There are a number of possible illnesses that precipitate hypoglycemia. Some are serious. Some are curable. All deserve specific treatment beyond staying away from sugar and entering upon a lifetime of eating small and frequent meals.

In summary, if you feel there is reason to think you have hypoglycemia, you should see an appropriate physician, ideally an endocrinologist, and take the appropriate tests and, if necessary, the proper treatment. Someone who is phobic will have to enter into exposure therapy in any case. There is no connection between agoraphobia and hypoglycemia except that the symptoms of one are vaguely suggestive of the other.

Mitral Valve Prolapse

The mitral valve is a valve between the left atrium of the heart and the left ventricle, two chambers of the heart. In 5 to 10 percent of the population, or even more, the leaflets of the valve billow, or bend, in an exaggerated movement during ventricular contraction. Most of these people have no symptoms at all from this condition, suggesting that MVP (mitral valve prolapse) may in most cases be simply a normal variant, particularly among women, in whom it seems to be more common. The diagnosis is made, sometimes with difficulty, on the basis of auscultory findings determined on examination with a stethoscope and also the heart's appearance on echocardiography. This illness, if that is what it is, is of such little apparent significance that it has only been discovered and defined in recent years.

The two most common symptoms of MVP are palpitations and chest pain—both common features of anxiety. The chest pain is usually described as sharp and sudden and may last for hours or longer. Occasionally it occurs with exertion and may suggest angina, the pain of coronary insufficiency. The true origin of the pain is unknown but may relate to certain skeletal abnormalities of the chest wall that often accompany this condition. The palpitations that many persons with MVP complain of may stem from occasional extra beats or a run of fast beats. Sometimes they are due to no more than a heightened awareness of an apparently normal heartbeat. There are, *very rarely*, possible complications of MVP, including infection on the mitral valve leaflets; to prevent this some doctors recommend antibiotics before undergoing dental procedures. *However, the great majority of people with MVP have none of these complaints or any others throughout their lives.* Those who do have chest pain or cardiac arrhythmias are treated readily and successfully with a variety of drugs. What, then, is the relationship between this very common and usually not at all serious cardiac abnormality and that other very common condition, agoraphobia?

People who are anxious or panicky often demonstrate a preoccupation with their health and in particular with their heart since that seems the most vital of the vital organs. "Soldier's heart" is a syndrome marked by fatigue, hyperventilation, dizziness, palpitations, shortness of breath, chest pain, and apprehension, and it is common in civilian life as well. These symptoms are thought to be of emotional origin, and yet they overlap with those of a variety of organic cardiac diseases, muscular disorders of the chest wall, esophageal diseases, and a number of other illnesses —and certainly mitral valve prolapse. It seems reasonable to wonder, therefore, if some of these people are responding to a subtle but real underlying physical illness such as MVP. A different hypothesis being investigated currently suggests that both MVP and panic disorder stem from the same basic cause: a dysfunction of the autonomic nervous system. In support of this idea, a number of studies have been reported in which there was a high incidence of MVP in patients who suffered panic attacks and were phobic. In the early studies, reporting *in sum* no more than fifty patients, this figure reached 50 percent. As usual, when other investigators pursued this new inquiry, these original significant findings began to look less significant. The most recent studies, including one performed at the White Plains Hospital Phobia Clinic, suggest that the prevalence of MVP in phobic patients is little if at all above what would be expected in an ordinary population.* Should it turn out, though, on still further investigation that there is indeed such an association, a ready explanation suggests itself: Phobics often show a concern about physical health even prior to developing their phobias. It is easy to understand how such a person suddenly experiencing an irregularity of heartbeat or pain in the area of the heart—from whatever cause—might develop a full-blown panic attack and as a result set in motion the process by which he develops a phobia. If so, MVP might reasonably be considered a precipitant of a phobia although not really a direct cause, any more than acid indigestion, for example, which also provokes chest pain and is also especially common among phobics, should be regarded as a cause of their condition.

* See the Appendix.

There is no evidence that MVP alters the course of a phobia. Someone so affected has panic attacks that are no more or less distressing than someone without MVP. His illness is not likely to be longer or more severe. He is no more or less likely to respond to tranquilizers, antidepressants, or exposure therapy, although the side effects of the antidepressants, almost always troublesome to phobics anyway, may require special attention since they affect cardiac conduction time. There is a class of drugs, the beta-blockers, that are effective in treating both the chest pain and the irregular heartbeat of MVP, although, as indicated previously, most of the time no treatment other than reassurance is necessary. These are drugs, incidentally, that had a vogue a number of years ago in the treatment of anxiety since they are supposed to block the physical signs of anxiety such as hyperventilation, palpitation, and trembling. As happened previously, though, with other drugs such as the major tranquilizers and then the minor tranquilizers, an early enthusiasm faded with time and more experience. Phobics taking the beta-blockers complain that the outward signs of anxiety are lessened, but they feel "just as panicky inside." Mitral valve prolapse in any case should not be a source of concern. It is a benign condition for the most part and readily managed.

In summary, if you are like most phobics—or even like most people in general—you will try to make sense out of your various physical symptoms by attributing them to one or another illness that you may have read or heard about. But try not to jump to conclusions. To someone not trained in medicine, it seems like every illness merges into every other. For reasons described in this chapter, even professionals are sometimes misled. If you have physical symptoms, you should see your doctor. That is the commonsense message of this chapter. But you cannot allow the search for an underlying physical cause of agoraphobia to distract you indefinitely from engaging in an exposure therapy.

Chapter 9

AFTER RECOVERY

Feelings serve a purpose, even very unpleasant feelings such as fear. They are a goad to action. For example, someone who is being treated rudely—or frustrated in any other way—is *supposed* to get angry. The subjective sense of being angry shows outwardly in a raised voice and an angry expression. A message is communicated of a particular kind of distress, and along with it a demand for attention. Other people respond, to a greater or lesser extent, by refraining from doing whatever was objectionable. Those who have trouble getting angry have trouble influencing the people around them. Every other feeling can be shown similarly to be useful. Joy and affection serve to tie people together, especially families. Sadness, such as homesickness, represents loss and is a reminder to make up that loss in some way. Grief occurs when the loss is too extreme to redress. Anxiety is the price for anticipating difficulties. It serves to preserve the individual, just as sexual feelings serve to preserve the species. Fear is perhaps the easiest emotion to understand. In the face of an immediate danger, animals, including human beings, demonstrate a "fight or flight" reaction. Along with the subjective sensation of fear there occurs a complicated physiological response that serves to prepare the individual for immediate action: muscles tense, respiration and heart rate increase, the blood pressure rises. The mouth becomes dry and digestion is disturbed, sometimes by cramps and the immediate urge to defecate. More subtle hormonal changes occur. And this same complicated response takes place whether someone is threatened by an angry boss, a gang of toughs in an alleyway, or a charging elephant. A dispute with a spouse, a school examination, a scary movie, a sudden injury—all circumstances that are frightening—set in motion the same train of physical changes, although to a varying extent depending on just how threatened the person feels. Each of these physical changes contributes to an ability to handle stress. They are aspects of heightened alertness and a physical readiness to respond decisively and promptly. They are normal. Drugs or other substances that interfere with their appearance also interfere with the ability to react.

But can anxiety become so severe that it interferes with the ability to cope? Is that panic? Yes. Fear, like other emotions, is a helpful response to ordinary circumstances, but in a situation where it is not possible to fight or take flight, the body's reaction to danger seems exaggerated and prolonged. Those who endured trench warfare found themselves troubled with emotional symptoms—shaking, sleeplessness, heightened sensitivity to lights and sounds, and so on—in addition to having to worry about falling shells. Panic occurs when the danger seems imminent and overwhelming—and unavoidable. In the case of shell shock it is more the situation itself that is abnormal than the emotional response to it.

However, there are times when the circumstances are ordinary and the person's response is abnormal. Such is the case in panic disorders. Someone standing in line at a bank or driving through a tunnel, in no apparent danger even by his own account, suddenly feels terrified and experiences all the physiological changes that accompany fear. For this remarkable phenomenon there are two different possible explanations:

1. Such a person is born with a special sensitivity, mediated perhaps through some limb of the central nervous system or endocrine system, and so overreacts, somewhat in the way a loudspeaker gives off a screech if the volume is set too high. The fact that panic disorders and the agoraphobia usually accompanying them run in families might seem explainable if the underlying disability turns out to be genetic. It is possible some such definable hypersensitivity will be found some day, but the evidence for it now is unconvincing. Neither would such a built-in weakness explain why someone would live to his mid-twenties or thirties without giving any sign of it, enter into a period of four or five years of being grossly symptomatic—feeling anxious most of the time and panicky at least once every day—and nevertheless, after proper treatment, continue the rest of his life without any symptoms.

2. The second explanation, put forward as the thesis of this book, is that the panicky person on some fundamental level *misunderstands* his circumstances and feels himself to be in acute danger when there is no objective danger, none even that *he* can see. Along the way of growing up he has learned, usually from his parents, that the world is a dangerous place. Even physical health, taken for granted by everyone else, is seen as precarious. Therefore, in order to ward off calamity, it is necessary to be always on guard. As a result, certain places, even certain feelings, become frightening. After a while even the feeling of being frightened becomes frightening. The panic attack appears at a particular time, perhaps, because of a particular stress —unfortunately usually too subtle to recognize immediately. From then on the generalized wariness such people have of the world centers on a fear of the panic attacks themselves, on the effect they have on physical and mental health and on every other aspect of life.

By this explanation, then, a phobia is an avoidance response to a nonexistent danger. It is the result of a *mistake in learning*. Treatment, therefore, is a learning or relearning process. The phobic must learn, first, that the panic attacks are not in and of themselves dangerous and, second, that the illusion of being trapped and helpless, whether in a tunnel or an airplane, is no more than that—an illusion. Nothing else is required for the cure of a phobia. To achieve that cure, the phobic person must develop an *active* stance in keeping with the fight-or-flight reaction, rather than waiting passively and helplessly for his feelings to subside.

Something much more desirable but impossible to achieve during an eight-week exposure therapy—or any other brief method of treatment—is a change of perspective on life itself. There are phobics who recover completely from their illness and live thereafter as successfully as anyone. But for many, the tendency to worry and be wary unnecessarily outlasts the phobia itself and can make everything—work, marriage, and especially bringing up children—a struggle. It is part of the bedrock of personality and changes slowly when it changes at all. It is a point of view that summarizes to a kind of philosophy of life:

Since the world is treacherous—by this way of thinking—one must always be alert to the possibility of injury or illness. New business ventures are likely to fail. New relationships are likely to founder. New places threaten vague and shadowy dangers rather than promising excitement or the chance to learn something new. Children must be guarded against all the physical and emotional dangers that loom in imagination. Hidden not very far below the surface of these mundane fears are the more profound fears of helplessness and loneliness.

Also, by this account, any kind of weakness is shameful; since any thought or feeling or behavior might be construed by *someone* as weakness, it is best that others, especially strangers, should know as little about one as possible. "It's none of their business" is the refrain repeated over and over again as instruction for everyone in the family. No other reason is offered to explain keeping silent. Even one's manner of speech and behavior needs to be controlled carefully lest some embarrassing feeling show through.

Most of all it is always important to worry and watch out in order to be prepared for any sudden mishap or misadventure.

What sort of life do these attitudes imply? It is a narrow, constrained existence in which the individual strives primarily to feel secure. Everything else is subordinated to the wish for safety. Relationships with parents, often ambivalent, are maintained very closely into the years of adulthood, although sometimes marked on both sides by guilt and resentment. A spouse is chosen sometimes solely because he or she seems "stable." Employment is chosen because it is safely within the individual's capacity and therefore does not threaten failure, or simply because it is nearby. Often such a job is kept long after it has proven to be unsatisfactory, unchallenging, or uninteresting. In all matters, the familiar is chosen over the unknown. The personality of such a person is inhibited: shy, self-conscious, anxious to please. He tries to contain his feelings, especially his aggressive urges. He is easily embarrassed, made to feel guilty, and depressed in addition to being frightened. He is seemingly faithful forever to his parents' image of how he should be.

This is by no means necessarily a miserable life. There is room for satisfaction and achievement. And pleasure. But it is not everything life can be. It is not an adventure.

Someone who sees the world the way it really is, on the other hand, has little reason to be afraid. Consequently, he can look forward enthusiastically to new places and new experiences. Although recognizing that disappointment and failure are inevitable occasionally, the risk does not seem so great or the disappointment so awful that he is deterred. The prospect of meeting new people is inviting. Social activities in general are fun. Whether or not to change jobs is a decision made only on the merits of the respective jobs and not on the basis of extraneous issues. Such a person is self-confident at work as he is in most places. He is assertive and direct. And open. Because he knows that certain important people respect him—such as his family and friends, and employer, perhaps—he does not have to worry about what others think. Rather than living by his parents' standards, he has developed his own values and his own ways of doing things. In short, he is independent. Since he lives up to his own standards, he does not customarily feel guilty, and he is not often embarrassed. If he does feel fear or anger or any other emotion, he can express it freely, *but he need not be ruled by it.* Even though the thought of giving a business presentation is frightening, for example, he may choose to give it anyway if he feels that doing so is in his best interest. Most of all he is a person who enjoys today and expects to enjoy whatever tomorrow may bring.

Perhaps no one can live up to this idealized portrait of a happy, mature person. Someone who is self-confident most of the time will be uneasy or self-conscious on certain occasions. No one is entirely free of self-doubts. To that extent it is natural to want to feel secure. But the struggle to be safe and secure, to be free of anxiety, is not enough reason to justify living from day to day. The phobic—or ex-phobic—cannot be happy for long sitting in front of a fireplace, however peacefully. Life is supposed to be exhilarating, at least some of the time. Phobics often discover that once they have recovered, those activities that were most frightening are now most pleasurable. A person who used to be afraid of driving finds himself getting in the car whenever he wants to be alone. A man who was once afraid of skiing becomes a downhill racer. These startling changes, unfortunately, do not by themselves change a basically pessimistic view of the world into one that is optimistic, nor do they encourage someone who is preoccupied with himself to get more involved with others. Yet that is what each person must do. Fulfillment is more than the avoidance of certain unpleasant feelings or circumstances. It is a commitment to other people and purposes outside of oneself.

This is an argument, then, for continuing past the point of recovery from a phobia. The practice of challenging one's fears that is the basis of exposure therapy is a reasonable strategy for coping with other more realistic threats. The danger of getting fired from a job, for instance, is managed best by confronting it directly, by talking to the employer and, perhaps, by looking for other work. Whether it is learning how to swim or learning how to address a group, both scary in their way, a determined, step-by-step effort usually brings success—as it does in overcoming a phobia. Being open with others, crucial to the success of exposure therapy, is important for everyone in developing close relationships and in being able to see oneself accurately through the eyes of others. These healthy attitudes are fostered by treatment but require further effort even after treatment is finished. Still, they bear on the final goal of every therapy: an independent, assertive, joyful life.

Appendix:
Examples of Tools *

TOOLS OF ROTE

1. *Tasting or eating* crackers, candy, ice cream, hot peppers, or chewing gum.
2. *Smelling* perfume or smelling salts.
3. *Listening* to the radio—talk shows in particular.
4. *Watching*, attending to, or keeping track of people, traffic lights, the musical cadence of a train, planes landing and taking off, and nearby conversations.
5. *Feeling* a pebble in a shoe, the tines of a comb, the sharp edge of keys, the slap of a rubber band, ice cubes, the wetness of a towelette, a pinch, a cold shower, a hot bath, the strong breeze that comes through a car window, the texture of clothing.
6. *Reciting* poetry or the alphabet backwards, repeating telephone numbers, remembering the names of classmates, favorite movies, or flavors of ice cream; adding up the numbers on a license plate; counting telephone poles or cracks in the sidewalk; practicing writing neatly; cooking familiar foods; singing or humming familiar songs; exercising; washing dishes; scrubbing the floor; washing a car; kicking a stone or an acorn; tying shoelaces; doodling; dancing; gardening; or running a finger down a list of tools.

TOOLS OF CONCENTRATION

1. *Entering into conversation:* asking directions, the time, or any other question. Making telephone calls, arguing, speaking into a tape recorder.

* The tools mentioned here have been invented by different phobic patients or phobia aides and have been found to be helpful. Obviously, their number can be expanded indefinitely.

2. *Making written notes* of changing levels of anxiety, of thoughts and feelings, or progress made so far. Writing letters.

3. *Timing* panic attacks, exposure to the phobic situation, intervals before someone comes, or the period between other events.

4. *Calculating* the amount of a purchase, the length of a trip, the number of trees along a particular route, the speed of a vehicle, the interest payments over the life of a home mortgage, the thirteen multiplication table, the expenses of having a child, the speed with which someone waiting on line is moving. Or counting backwards from a hundred by sevens.

5. *Reading* novels, newspapers, magazines, grocery lists, letters, notes made ahead of time, or this book.

6. *Working:* household work, for example, if it requires thought, but work upon which one depends for a living is best.

7. *Planning* the day's activities, the week's activities, how to manage tomorrow's practice session, or an appropriate reward for successfully completing the session.

8. *Playing* cards or other games, especially with other people; for example, chess or checkers. Playing a sport. Playing with children.

9. *Playing* a harmonica or any other musical instrument.

10. *Engaging in creative activities:* painting, writing verse, ceramics.

11. *Working out puzzles:* crossword puzzles, jigsaw puzzles, pocket puzzles, word puzzles, such as listing all the words that can be found in another word or all the words that begin with an S and end with a T. Spelling words backwards. Determining by feel alone which of a pocketful of keys will fit which locks.

12. *Engaging in sex* or even sexual daydreams.

13. *Investigating the causes* of the panic by keeping track of the thoughts, perceptions, circumstances, fantasies, and activities that directly preceded its appearance.

The following activities, if they can be described as such, do not usually work very well:

1. Sitting quietly
2. Resting in bed
3. Standing stiffly
4. Gritting teeth or clenching fists
5. Breathing deeply
6. Pacing
7. Holding someone's hand
8. Breathing into a paper bag
9. Just plain trying to relax or think "happy thoughts"

These all present one problem or another. Either they heighten the phobic's passivity, aggravate his symptoms directly, or make him feel foolish. Even so, they work sometimes. What matters in the final analysis is the determination with which *any* activity is pursued.

In actual practice, the tools a particular person may use are likely to be only a few. The following are illustrations of how particular patients dealt with various phobic situations and the panicky feelings likely to occur in those settings:

TOOLS OF ROTE

TOOLS OF CONCENTRATION

Elevators

1. Eating a chocolate bar
2. Staring at panelling or running a hand along a rail
3. Stamping a foot lightly on the floor

1. Reviewing a diary of previous visits to the elevator
2. Writing a description of the ride in the diary.

Trains

1. Taking an inventory of the contents of a pocketbook
2. Chewing licorice candy
3. Fiddling with a child's puzzle

1. Talking to anyone or asking the conductor questions
2. Composing stories about the other people sitting in the train

Restaurants

1. Drawing designs on a napkin with a fork
2. Drinking ice water
3. Washing hands in very cold water

1. Adding up the prices on the menu
2. Telephoning friends
3. Timing the panicky feelings

Automobiles

1. Feeling the bumps on the steering wheel
2. Cleaning out the glove compartment
3. Counting the number of out-of-state license plates on the road

1. Speaking to a passenger or into a tape recorder
2. Keeping track of the minutes traveled and the miles yet to go

Airplanes

1. Counting the passengers or the steps from the front of the plane to the back
2. Walking back and forth along the aisle

1. Talking to the stewardess
2. Doing paperwork from the office
3. Reading magazines

Heights

1. Looking at people who are standing nearby and also, paradoxically, looking at the horizon
2. Scuffling feet
3. Playing with a wristwatch band

1. Timing the panicky feelings
2. Making written record of the anxious feelings as they rise and fall
3. Talking

Walking a Distance

1. Counting steps
2. Kicking a pebble
3. Counting passing cars

1. Timing the walk or the panicky feelings
2. Figuring how much longer today's walk is than yesterday's, and at that rate of improvement, how much longer it will be before the walk can be extended indefinitely

Parties

1. Eating constantly
2. Washing hands and face
3. Going through the contents of a purse

1. Telephoning home
2. Preparing food in the kitchen
3. Talking to a particular friend

Church

1. Counting all the people in attendance, then all the women parishioners, then all the children
2. Feeling the wood grain of the pew
3. Silently humming a favorite hymn

1. Reading the stories in the Bible
2. Timing the length of the sermon or of other parts of the service

Beauty Parlors

1. Listening to music
2. Chewing gum
3. Sipping juice

1. Solving crossword puzzles
2. Talking to the beautician
3. Underlining a textbook

Department Stores

1. Examining prices
2. Feeling clothing materials
3. Looking at flower arrangements

1. Asking questions about the merchandise
2. Adding up purchases
3. Taking detailed notes of the experience

Movie Theaters

1. Eating candy
2. Playing with a pocket comb
3. Counting loose change

1. Telephoning home
2. Talking to the person who sells candy
3. Figuring household expenses for the rest of the week

Open Spaces

1. Jogging and measuring distances by counting steps
2. Repeating the Lord's Prayer or reading down a list of "things to do"

1. Working a keyring puzzle
2. Drawing pictures of the surroundings
3. Talking to a friend

Classrooms

1. Penciling in squares randomly on graph paper
2. Playing with plastic putty
3. Leafing through a book

1. Taking very detailed lecture notes
2. Drawing cartoons
3. Adding up prime numbers

Hospitals

1. Counting steps
2. Smelling an artificial flower
3. Snapping a rubber band attached to a wrist

1. Asking questions of the hospital staff
2. Timing the visit and the panicky feelings if they come
3. Calling someone on the telephone

Alone at Home

1. Taking brief walks in the garden
2. Cleaning the house
3. Washing dishes

1. Telephoning friends and family
2. Outlining the following week's practice sessions
3. Balancing the checkbook

NAME _____ PLAN FOR THIS COMING WEEK   DATE _____

MONDAY	
TUESDAY	
WEDNESDAY	
THURSDAY	
FRIDAY	
SATURDAY	
SUNDAY	
WORK SESSION WITH HELPER	

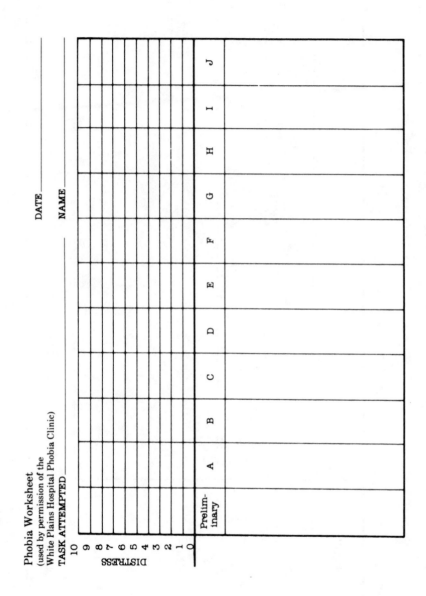

Phobia Worksheet
(used by permission of the
White Plains Hospital Phobia Clinic)

DATE

NAME

TASK ATTEMPTED

DISTRESS

	A	B	C	D	E	F	G	H	I	J
10										
9										
8										
7										
6										
5										
4										
3										
2										
1										
0										
Prelim- inary										

CONCOMITANT INTERNAL EVENTS (thoughts, feelings, images, impulses, bodily sensations)

Preliminary.

A.

B.

C.

D.

E.

F.

G.

H.

I.

J.

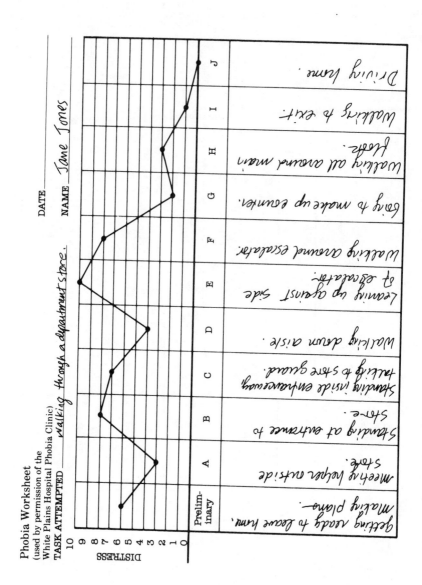

Phobia Worksheet
(used by permission of the
White Plains Hospital Phobia Clinic)

DATE

NAME Jane Jones

TASK ATTEMPTED Walking through a department store.

DISTRESS

	Preliminary	A	B	C	D	E	F	G	H	I	J

Getting ready to leave home. Making plans.

Meeting helper outside store.

Standing at entrance to store.

Standing inside entranceway. Talking to store guard.

Walking down aisle.

Leaning up against side of escalator.

Walking around escalator.

Going to make-up counter.

Walking all around main floor.

Walking to exit.

Driving home.

CONCOMITANT INTERNAL EVENTS (thoughts, feelings, images, impulses, bodily sensations)

Preliminary:

A. Relieved to see helper. In case something happens, she'll know what to do. Feel shaky and sweaty, hopeful though. Maybe I'll be able to stop again.

B. Scared. People rushing in and out. Feel light-headed, short of breath. Dizzy a little. Tempted not to try. Don't want to give up, though, before I begin!?

C. Talking helps. Still shaky, but not as bad as I thought. Bright lights reassuring, but too noisy. Trying to catch my breath.

D. Feel like I'm floating. Hope I don't fall. As long as I keep walking. I'm okay. Why can't I just be calm, like these other people?

E. Suddenly, I remember panic attack I had last year, standing right here, and right away I'm panicky again. Heart beating a mile a minute. I think everyone is looking at me. Feel like I'm going to faint? I want to leave!

F. Talking to helper. She reminds me of tools. Unfolding piece of paper in my hand makes me feel a little better. Try to time panic, but too nervous to concentrate. Still a little calmer.

G. This can't be as bad as I thought. Smell of perfume distracts me. I see my face in the mirror and I look normal. Good feeling, except weak in legs.

H. Walking definitely helps. I feel like running. Helper makes jokes and I laugh. Feel trapped suddenly when a bunch of people crowd around.

I. I did it! Feeling of exhilaration. Tempted to stay longer. I don't notice my body at all.

J. Tired, but not nervous. Look forward to telling husband. Next time I'm going to the second floor!

TREATMENT RESOURCES

Information about local treatment facilities, newsletters, and home-centered or self-help treatment programs can be obtained from the officers of the Phobia Society of America listed below:

Regional Governors' Coordinator

Doreen Powell
Phobia Clinic
White Plains Hospital Medical Center
Davis Avenue at Post Road
White Plains, NY 10601
914-681-1078

Regional Governors

Region I: MD, DC, DE, NJ, PA, NY, CT, RI, VT, NH, ME, MA

Raymond A. Hornyak, Ph.D.
Clinical Director
TERRAP of Pennsylvania
918 Park Avenue
Pittsburgh, PA 15234
412-341-1162

Jo Ann Antonelli
Phobia Clinic
White Plains Hospital Medical Center
Davis Avenue at Post Road
White Plains, NY 10601
914-681-1078

Region II: OH, KY, IN, IL, WI, MI

Joel M. Kestenbaum, Ph.D.
5800 Monroe Street, Bldg. B
Sulvania, OH 43560
419-882-4624

Pat Foster
9302 N. Meridian Street
Suite 102
Indianapolis, IN 46260
317-253-3160

Region III: LA, MS, AL, GA, FL, SC, NC, VA, WV, TN

R. Reid Wilson, Ph.D.
Route 5, Box 214A
Chapel Hill, NC 27514

Region IV: ND, MN, SD, WY, CO, KS, OK, TX, NM, MO, IA, AR, NB

James O. Wilson, M.A.
Director
Center for Human Devel-
    opment and Phobia Cen-
    ter of the Southwest
12860 Hillcrest Road,
    Suite 119
Dallas, TX 75230
214-386-6327

Bob Handly
6526 Chevy Chase
Dallas, TX 75225
214-691-7485

Region V: AZ, CA, NV, UT, ID, OR, WA, MT

Joyce E. Kaplan, MFCC
Director, Phobia Treatment
    Center
3688 Mt. Diablo Blvd.
Lafayette, CA 94549
415-376-5530 (Office)
415-376-6714 (Home)

Chuck Wickstrand, MFCC
1811 Brentwood Road
Oakland, CA 94602
415-530-9434

A NOTE ON MITRAL VALVE PROLAPSE

An attempt was made through the White Plains Hospital Phobia Clinic to discover how many former patients had been determined to have mitral valve prolapse. They were asked to convey a questionnaire to their physicians. A covering letter explained, among other things, the variety of symptoms associated with MVP. Of 273 people queried in such a way, only 47 responded fully, suggesting that for the others the possibility of having MVP seemed too unlikely to justify visiting their doctors —or too threatening.

Of those who responded, 4 had MVP and 43 did not.

This is a proportion well within the range reported for the general population. Of an additional 32 patients reached by telephone, 31 felt they did not have MVP on the basis of their symptoms but had not necessarily seen their doctors.

RECOMMENDED READING

Chambless, D. L. and Goldstein, A. J., eds. *Agoraphobia: Multiple Perspectives on Theory and Treatment* (New York: John Wiley and Sons, 1982).

Dupont, R. L., ed. *Phobia: A Comprehensive Summary of Modern Treatments* (New York: Brunner Mazel, 1982).

Hardy, A. B. *Agoraphobia: Symptoms, Causes, Treatment.* Brochure. (Menlo Park, CA: Terrap, 1976).

Marks, I. M. *Living with Fear: Understanding and Coping with Anxiety* (New York: McGraw-Hill, 1978).

Weeks, C. *Simple Effective Treatment of Agoraphobia* (New York: Hawthorne Books, 1976).

Zane, M. D. *Your Phobia: Understanding Your Fears Through Contextual Therapy* (Washington, D. C.: American Psychiatric Press, 1984).

Bibliography

THE USE OF DRUGS

Garakani, H., et al. "Treatment of Panic Disorder with Imipramine Alone," *American Journal of Psychiatry* 141:446–48 (1984).

Gloger, S., et al. "Treatment of Spontaneous Panic Attacks with Chlomipramine," *American Journal of Psychiatry* 138:1215–17 (September 1981).

Gonzalez, E. R. "Panic Disorder May Respond to New Antidepressants." *Journal of American Medical Association* 248:3077–38, 3086–87 (December 17, 1982).

Hallstrom, C., et al. "Diazepam, Propranolol and Their Combination in the Management of Chronic Anxiety," *British Journal of Psychiatry* 139:417–21 (1981).

Heiser, J. F., and Defrancisco, D. "The Treatment of Pathological Panic States with Propranolol," *American Journal of Psychiatry* 133:1389–94 (1976).

Klein, D. F. "Delineation of Two Drug-Responsive Anxiety Syndromes," *Psychopharmacologia* 5:397–408 (1964).

Leckman, J., et al. "Panic Disorder and Major Depression," *Archives of General Psychiatry* 40:1055–60 (1983).

Lipsedge, M., et al. "The Management of Severe Agoraphobia: A Comparison of Iproniazid and Systematic Desensitization," *Psychopharmacologia* 32:67–80 (1973).

Marks, I. M. "Are There Anticompulsive or Antiphobic Drugs? Review of the Evidence," *British Journal of Psychiatry* 143:338–47 (1983).

Marks, I. M., et al. "Imipramine and Brief Therapist-Aided Exposure in Agoraphobics Having Self-Exposure Homework, *Archives of General Psychiatry* 40:153–162, (February 1983).

McNair, D. M., and Kahn, R. J. "Imipramine Compared with a Benzodiazepine for Agoraphobia. In *Anxiety: New Research and Changing Concepts*, edited by D. R. Klein and J. Rabkin. (New York: Raven Press, 1981), pp. 69–80.

Mountjoy, C. Q., et al. "A Clinical Trial of Phenelzine in Anxiety, Depressive and Phobic Neuroses," *British Journal of Psychiatry* 131:486–92 (1977).

Noyes, Jr., R., et al. "Diazepam and Propranolol in Panic Disorder and Agoraphobia," *Archives of General Psychiatry* 41 (3):287–92 (March 1984).

Shader, R, et al. "Panic Disorders: Current Perspectives," *Journal of Clinical Psychopharmacology* 2:(6 Supplement) 25–105 (December 1982).

Sheehan, D. V. "Current Perspectives in the Treatment of Panic and Phobia Disorders," *Drug Therapy* 12:58 (1982).

————. "Panic Attacks and Phobias," *New England Journal of Medicine* 307:156–58 (July 15, 1982).

Sheehan, D. V., et al. "Treatment of Endogenous Anxiety with Phobic Hysterical and Hypochondriacal Symptoms," *Archives of General Psychiatry* 37:51–9 (1980).

Shehi, M., and Patterson, W. M. "Treatment of Panic Attacks with Alprazolam and Propranolol," *American Journal of Psychiatry* 141:900–01 (1984).

Snaith, R. P. "A Study of Imipramine in the Treatment of Phobias," *British Journal of Psychiatry* 121:238–39 (August 1972).

Solyom, L., et al. "Behavior Therapy Versus Drug Therapy in the Treatment of Phobic Neurosis," *Canadian Psychiatric Association Journal* 18:25–32 (1973).

————. "Phenelzine and Exposure in the Treatment of Phobias," *Biological Psychiatry* 16:239–48 (1981).

Tyer, P., and Steinberg, D. "Symptomatic Treatment of Agoraphobia and Social Phobias: A Follow-up Study," *British Journal of Psychiatry* 127:163–68 (1975).

Zitrin, C.M., et al. "Behavior Therapy, Supportive Psychotherapy, Imipramine and Phobias," *Archives of General Psychiatry* 35:307–16 (1978).

————. "Treatment of Agoraphobia with Group Exposure in Vivo and Imipramine," *Archives of General Psychiatry* 37:63–72 (1980).

HYPOGLYCEMIA AND PHOBIAS

Editorial: Gastineau, C. "Is Reactive Hypoglycemia a Clinical Entity?" *Mayo Clinic Proc.* 58:545–49 (1983).

Editorial: "Statement on Hypoglycemia," *Journal of American Medical Association* 223:682 (1973).

Special report from the American Diabetes Association, the Endocrine Society, and the American Medical Association. "Statement on Hypoglycemia," *Diabetes* 22:137 (1973).

Anderson, R. W., and Lev-Ran, Arye. "Hypoglycemia: The Standard and the Fiction," *Psychosomatics* 26 (1): 38–47 (1985).

Brody, S., and Wolitzky, D. "Lack of Mood Changes Following Sucrose Loading," *Psychosomatics* 24 (2):155–57, 161–62 (February 1983).

Cahill, Jr., G. F., and Soeldner, J. S. "A Non-editorial on Nonhypoglycemia." Editorial. *New England Journal of Medicine* 291:905–06 (1974).

Charles, M. A., et al. "Comparison of Oral Glucose Tolerance Tests and Mixed Meals in Patients with Apparent Idiopathic Postabsorptive Hypoglycemia: Absence of Hypoglycemia After Meals," *Diabetes* 30:465–70 (1981).

Gorman, J. M., et al. "Hypoglycemia and Panic Attacks," *American Journal of Psychiatry* 141:101–02 (January 1984).

Green, T. "Reactive Hypoglycemia: Current Diagnosis and Treatment," *Journal of AOA* 80 (12):827–30 (1981).

Hofeldt, F. D., et al. "Post-Prandial Hypoglycemia: Fact or Fiction?" *Journal of American Medical Association* 233:1309 (1975).

Hogan, M., et al. "Oral Glucose Tolerance Test Compared with a Mixed Meal in the Diagnosis of Reactive Hypoglycemia: A Caveat on Stimulation," *Mayo Clinic Proceedings* 58: 491–96 (August 1983).

Johnson, D. D., et al. "Reactive Hypoglycemia," *Journal of American Medical Association* 243:1151–55 (1980).

Lev-Ran, A., and Anderson, R. W. "The Diagnosis of Postprandial Hypoglycemia," *Diabetes* 30:996–99 (1981).

Yager, J., and Young, R. T. "Non-Hypoglycemia is an Epidemic Condition," *New England Journal of Medicine* 291:907–08 (1974).

RELATIONSHIP OF DEPRESSION AND PHOBIAS

Bowen, R. C., and Kohout, J. "The Relationship Between Agoraphobia and Primary Affective Disorders," *Canadian Journal of Psychiatry* 24:317–22 (1979).

Crowe, R. R., et al. "A Family Study of Panic Disorder," *Archives of General Psychiatry* 40:1065–69 (1983).

Emmelkamp, P. M. G., and Kuipers, A. C. M. "Agoraphobia: A Follow Study Four Years After Treatment, *British Journal of Psychiatry* 134:352–55 (1979).

Hamilton, M. "Depression and Anxiety: A Clinical Viewpoint," *Psychiatry in the 80's* 1:4 (1983).

Leckman, J. F., et al. "Panic Disorder and Major Depression: Increased Risk of Depression, Alcoholism, Panic and Phobic Disorders in Families of Depressed Probands with Panic Disorder," *Archives of General Psychiatry* 40:1055–60 (1983).

Marks, I. M. "Phobic Disorders Four Years After Treatment," *British Journal of Psychiatry* 118:683–88 (1971).

Mathew, R. J., et al. "Vegetative Symptoms in Anxiety and Depression," *British Journal of Psychiatry* 141:162–65 (1982).

McNair, D. M., and Kahn, R. J. "Imipramine Compared with a Benzodiazepine for Agoraphobia." In *Anxiety: New Research and Changing Concepts*, edited by D. R. Klein and J. Rabkin. (New York: Raven Press, 1981), pp. 69–80.

Munjack, D. J., and Moss, H. B. "Affective Disorder and Alcoholism in Families of Agoraphobics," *Archives of General Psychiatry* 38:869–71 (1981).

Pollit, J., and Young, J. "Anxiety State or Marked Depression? A Study Based on the Action of Monoamine Oxidase Inhibitors," *British Journal of Psychiatry* 119:143–49 (1971).

Raskin, M., et al. "Panic and Generalized Anxiety Disorder: Developmental Antecedents and Precipitants," *Archives of General Psychiatry* 39:687–89 (1982).

Roth, M., et al. "Studies in the Classification of Affective Disorders. The Relationship Between Anxiety States and Depression Illnesses," *British Journal of Psychiatry* 121:147–61 (1972).

———. "Further Investigations into the Relationship Between Depressive Disorders and Anxiety States," *Pharmakopsychiatria. Neuropsychopharmakol* 15:135–41 (1982).

Sadler, J. Z., et al. "Secondary Agoraphobia: Two Case Reports," *Journal of Clinical Psychiatry* 45:482–83 (1984).

Schapira, K., et al. "The Prognosis of Affective Disorders: The Differentiation of Anxiety States from Depressive Illness," *British Journal of Psychiatry* 121: 175–81 (1972).

Van Valkenburg, et al. "Depressed Women with Panic Attacks," *Journal of Clinical Psychiatry* 45 (9): 367–69 (September 1984).

Weissman, M. M., et al. "Depression and Anxiety Disorders in Parents and Children," *Archives of General Psychiatry* 41:845–52 (1984).

MITRAL VALVE PROLAPSE AND PHOBIAS

Bondanlas, H., et al. "Mitral Valve Prolapse: A Marker for Anxiety or Overlapping Phenomenon?" *Psychopathology* 17 (Supplement 1):98–106 (1984).

Darsee, J. R., et al. "Prevalence of Mitral Valve Prolapse in Presumably Healthy Young Men," *Circulation* 59(4):619–22 (1979).

Dietch, J. T. "Diagnosis of Organic Anxiety Disorders," *Psychosomatics* 22 (8):661–69 (August 1981).

Falk, R. H., and Hood, Jr., W. B. "Mitral Valve Prolapse: Striking a Therapeutic Balance," *Drug Therapy* (September 1981): 125–34.

Flannery, J. G., and Szmuilowicz, J. "Psychiatric Implications of the Mitral Valve Prolapse Syndrome (MVPS)," *Canadian Journal of Psychiatry* 24:740–43 (1979).

Gelfand, M. L., et al. "Mitral Valve Systolic Click Syndrome," *A F P* 21 (5):135–41 (1980).

Gorman, J. M., et al. "Effect of Sodium Lactate on Patients with Panic Disorder and Mitral Valve Prolapse," *American Journal of Psychiatry* 138(2):247–49 (1981).

Hartman, N., et al. "Panic Disorder in Patients with Mitral Valve Prolapse," *American Journal of Psychiatry* 139:669–70 (1982).

Hendricks, C. W., and Usher, B. W. "Mitral Valve Prolapse: A Review," *Journal of the South Carolina Medical Association* (September 1979): 400–02.

Hickey, A. J., et al. "Independence of Mitral Valve Prolapse and Neurosis," *British Heart Journal* 50:333–36 (1983).

Jeresaty, R. M. *Mitral Valve Prolapse* (New York: Raven Press, 1979).

Kantor, J. S., et al. "Mitral Valve Prolapse Syndrome in Agoraphobic Patients," *American Journal of Psychiatry* 137 (4):467–69 (1980).

Kerber, R. E., et al. "Mitral Valve Prolapse Syndrome in Anxiety Neurosis," *American Heart Journal* 102:139 (1981).

Leatham, A., and Brigden, W. "Mild Mitral Regurgitation and the Mitral Prolapse Fiasco," *American Heart Journal* 99:659–64 (1980).

Markiewicz, W., et al. "Mitral Valve Prolapse in 100 Presumably Healthy Young Females," *Circulation* 53:464–73 (1976).

Mavissakalian, M., et al. "Mitral Valve Prolapse and Agoraphobia," *American Journal of Psychiatry* 140(12): 1612–14 (1983).

Mehta, D., and Mehta, S. "Psychiatric Symptoms and Mitral Valve Prolapse Syndrome," *American Journal of Psychiatry* 135 (8): 1001–02 (1978).

Mills, P., et al. "Long-Term Prognosis of Mitral Valve Prolapse," *New England Journal of Medicine* 297:13–18 (1977).

Naggar, C. Z. "The Mitral Valve Prolapse Syndrome, Spectrum and Therapy," *Medical Clinics of North America* 63 (2):337–53 (1979).

Oakley, C. M. "Mitral Valve Prolapse: Harbinger of Death or Variant of Normal," *British Medical Journal* 288:6434:1853–54 (June 23, 1984).

Pariser, S. F., et al. "Mitral Valve Prolapse Syndrome and Anxiety Neurosis/Panic Disorder," *American Journal of Psychiatry* 135 (2):246–47 (1978).

———. "Panic Attacks: Diagnostic Evaluations of 17 Patients," *American Journal of Psychiatry* 136 (1):105–06 (1979).

Procacci, D. M., et al. "Prevalence of Clinical Mitral Valve Prolapse in 1,169 Young Women," *New England Journal of Medicine* 294:1086–88 (1976).

Schlant, R. C., et al. "Mitral Valve Prolapse," *D M* 26:3-51, (July 1980).

Shear, M. K., et al. "Low Prevalence of Mitral Valve Prolapse in Patients with Panic Disorders," *American Journal of Psychiatry* 141 (2):302–03 (2) (February 1984).

Szmuilowicz, J., and Flannery, J. G. "Mitral Valve Prolapse Syndrome and Psychological Disturbance," *Psychosomatics* 21 (5):419–21 (1980).

Venkatesh, A., et al. "Mitral Valve Prolapse in Anxiety Neurosis (Panic Disorder)," *American Heart Journal* 100 (3):302–05 (1980).

Weinstein, G., et al. "Anxiety and Mitral Valve Prolapse Syndrome," *Journal of Clinical Psychiatry* 43 (1):33–34 (1982).

Winkle, R. A., et al. "Propanolol for Patients with Mitral Valve Prolapse," *American Heart Journal* 93:422–27 (1977).

Index

Acrophobia, 3, 145–46
Agitated depression, 196–200
  antidepressant drugs and, 198,
    199–200
  endogenous depression and,
    197
  exposure therapy and, 198
  misdiagnosis and, 199
  panic attack symptoms and, 197–
    98
Agoraphobia:
  anxiety, pervasiveness of, 10–
    11
  case history, 4–9, 109–10, 127–
    28
  causes of, 15–24
  character and, 25–26
  chest pain and, 11
  course of illness, 14
  dangerous place, world seen as,
    18–19
  defined, 4
  dependent parent-child
    relationship and, 16–17
  depression and, 14–15
  distance distortions, 21
  dizziness and, 11
  elements characterizing, 10–13
  fear of fear and, 17
  feelings, loss of control over, 16–
    17
  flushing and, 12
  helplessness and, 12, 17
  heredity and, 15–16
  "lesser" phobias and, 10
  loss of control and, 12
  medication for, 50–54
  misconceptions of phobic, 22–24
  misdiagnosis and, 15
  mistaken ideas as basis for, 18–
    22
  motivation and, 25–26

pallor and, 12
palpitations and, 11
panic, fear of, 20–21
panic attacks and, 12–13
parents of phobics, 16
phobic avoidance, 13–15
physical health, preoccupation
  with, 19–20
shame and embarrassment
  over, 21–22
shortness of breath and, 11
"stuck points" and, 139–40
symptoms of anxiety, 11–12
time distortions, 21
treatment, 27–54
urge to withdraw and, 13
weakness and trembling, 11–12
Ailurophobia, 1
Airplane, first flight in, 90–92
Algophobia, 1
Alone. *See* Being alone, fear of
Alprazolam (Xanax), 52n
American Journal of Psychiatry,
  200n
Animal phobias, 2–3, 140–42, 151–
  52
Antidepressant drugs, 53, 198
Anxiety attacks, 6, 10–11
  pervasive anxiety feelings, 10–
    11
  See also Panic attacks; Panic
    attacks, fear of

Being alone, fear of, 70–71, 135–
  36
Bennion, Lynn, 202n
Betablockers, 206

*Caring: Home Treatment for the
  Emotionally Disturbed*
  (Neuman), 176n
Chest pain, 11, 204

235